CHANAKYA

The Guru of Governance

Publishers
PUSTAK MAHAL®
Administrative office and sale centre
J-3/16, Daryaganj, New Delhi-110002
☎ 011-23276539, 23272783, 23272784, 23260518
E-mail: info@pustakmahal.com • *Website:* www.pustakmahal.com

Branches
Bengaluru: ☎ 080-22234025, 40912845
E-mail: pustakmahalblr@gmail.com
Mumbai: ☎ 022-22010941, 22053387
E-mail: unicornbooksmumbai@gmail.com

ISBN 978-81-223-1010-8
Edition: 2020

Printed at: Ar Emm International, Delhi.

Dedication

To those who are young
and storing information in place of knowledge,
and to those who will be young
and will strive for knowledge,
and to my sons
Mitresh Manu and Arya Priyamber
who need Chanakya the most!

— **Prof. Shrikant Prasoon**

CONTENTS

CONTENTS

Preface

There was a time when I was facing many difficulties in life and was badly in need of correct and practical solutions. I tried different options, searched at many places, talked to all wise men but the solution eluded me. Then, one day I picked up Chanakya's *Niti Shastra*. I started reading the book with a hope, and was delighted to find that each of my problems was discussed and easy solutions were printed in it in bold letters.

At that time, I wrote two articles in Hindi — "Chanakya Ki Drishti Mein Nari" and "Chanakya Ki Vyawaharikta". Six years after that incident, I was assigned to write this book *Rule the World — The way I did* by Shri Ram Avtar Gupta. I got an opportunity to know that energetic man and his powerful mind better. The book in itself is an effort to explore the multifarious talents of Chanakya.

I sincerely hope that reading this book gives you both pleasure and wisdom.

— Prof. Shrikant Prasoon

SECTION – I

Chanakya : The Man and the Legend

A Peerless Personality

Chanakya is Chanakya, the only one of his kind in the known human history. There is no other similar personality. He is unique, individualistic and egocentric. Such a personality cannot be described in words. Even hundreds of world's great thinkers of different field combined together cannot come closer to his wisdom. He was not a mystic, but he had a mysterious nature and personality. He was a theorist and a practical man of the world: expert and adapt at both the ends and in both the fields.

Chanakya meticulously, diligently and intelligently laid down the 'tough principles', popularised them and followed them himself. He practised all that he asked others to follow.

He had a simple and lively childhood. But the moment he grew young and acquired adequate knowledge, he grew in strength and eagerly showed the world what he was and what he wanted to make the world. Rest of his life is known for his eccentricity, courage, wisdom and success.

Chanakya was an outcome of the events and tide of the time and he powerfully controlled both the tidal waves and the tempestuous events. Life was not very difficult for him but he deliberately and laboriously made it hard, tough and very difficult to live. He set such targets and standards for himself and the world around him that nothing remained easier for anyone concerned. All his tasks and promises were challenging. Ironically enough, he accomplished them all one by one.

He was a man of principles and he laid them down in black and white for others to know, learn and follow. He had all the great 'Ds' and showed the world that a man could possess them all and use them well. He was disciplined, determined, dedicated, and so on. He was a creative and constructive genius. Because he demolished a powerful kingdom and annihilated a living dynasty, he is often treated as a destructive power. But this is not the reality. The opposite is the truth. He demolished a stale kingdom and an arrogant dynasty and established a fresh dynasty and created a powerful and united kingdom. He created, tested and established a great system of governance for the good of the masses. Of course, the administration was centralised in a few strong hands but it was for all and not only for the benefit of those selected and lucky few.

Chanakya was a great friend to a friend but he was not a friendly figure. He was the most poisonous enemy, deadly and imperishable. He was a great guardian. He could go to any extent to save his wards, but he was never a father-like figure. He was too emotional to be taken as gentle. He was a teacher par excellence. He taught everything and expected that his teachings should be observed in detail. He was a pragmatic adviser and forced others to follow his advice meticulously well and in painstaking detail. He was not easy and would not make the path easier for anyone. He had one great motto — the higher the ambition the greater must be the effort to fulfil it.

Though known for his anger, Chanakya was a very cool-headed man. He maintained his cool and moved his pieces in a very calculated way. He was a great teacher because he was a great learner himself. He learnt from his own and others' mistakes and follies and taught general, obvious, intricate, mysterious and hidden truths for correct understanding, true judgement and astonishing success in professional and personal life.

Chanakya was an ambiguous and multifaceted personality. He had many names and numerous qualities, which are distinct and paranormal. He was a simple man, a great pupil, a loving son, an honourable teacher, a powerful minister, a mysterious strategist, a dangerous antagonist, a wild fighter, a diligent planner, an able executive and an honest adviser. He fixed difficult targets for self and for others, spent and utilised all the resources, physical energy and mental acumen to achieve them. He knew his responsibilities well and made honest and utmost efforts to fulfil them. This is what he taught the world — to do the best under every favourable or deadly circumstance.

Chanakya should be known, read and followed, not for the sake of studying his age, aspects of the ancient period, or history, economics or politics. He must be read and understood well for knowing modern men and women, the intriguing facts of life, the society and economy in general, the administration and the execution of particular plans and for overall planning and greater success.

Chanakya is needed most in this age when globalisation has firmly fixed its roots and is spreading far and wide. Luckily Management Universities and Institutes are now laying adequate stress on his principles, theories, doctrines, observations and practical approach. All ambitious people should know and follow him for instant success and immense satisfaction. The devotees, businessmen, teachers, executives, officers, statesmen and politicians must read and know Chanakya for correct understanding, timely implementation of plans and desired success in their respective fields. Remember, Chanakya was a practical man of the world; he was the most successful minister, a powerful commander and an alert executive, all in one. His teachings can change a simple soul into a 'global figure', because of their practicality and prolificacy.

Believe it, Chanakya was and will always remain MODERN. He will always remain alive in his thoughts, and will continue to awaken sleeping and depressed minds. So, get started, wake up and move ahead with his priceless teachings.

The Mysterious Life of Chanakya

Chanakya, the greatest political and social thinker of all times, was born and lived in India between 350 BC and 275 BC. It is usually said that he belonged to the 4th century BC. He was not only the wisest and most powerful person of his time but also a genius who was known for making a king and an empire. He united the whole of India under one ruler, Chandragupta Maurya and made the Mauryan Dynasty a golden period in the history of ancient India. He was truly dedicated to his ideals, ethics and duties. He followed humanism as described in the Indian scriptures. He fearlessly fought his way through dense, dark, dreary and divided kingdoms and society.

Chanakya was the son of Chanak. It is certain he came from Taxila. He might have belonged to Taxila or might have only taken his education from there. In the opinion of some scholars, Chanak lived with his family in the suburban areas of Magadh, most probably in the north of Ganga. Such a conclusion is drawn from the fact that Chanakya gave more time to the northern area of Patliputra, Chanaki garh in the West Champaran, which had a direct link with Patliputra through Lauria, Kesariya and Hajipur. It is claimed that if a lamp was shown on the Chanaki garh, the light was visible from a similar garh at Hajipur, and it may have been visible from Patliputra. This cannot be claimed now for that place is no longer there.

This peerless personality is always described as:

A Black Brahmin: He was black for he was probably from Kerala, black from outside and from inside a Brahmin who was pure, sublime and illuminating at his heart. His inner purity could purify others and show them true and convenient path. It was not really the ugliness of his countenance, but the roughness and toughness of knowledge, which never comes easily. Regarding his colour, a *shloka* can be cited which claims that a Brahmin represents his age, nature and colour. In *Satyug* and *Treta*, it was milky white, in *Dwaper* wheatish and in *Kaliyug*, it was black. The nature of an age was reflected by the colour of a Brahmin.

Yuge yuge tu ye dharmā teshu dhameshu ye dwijāh
Teshām nindā nā kartavyā yuga rupāhi brāhmanā

A Lean and Thin Person: This is a proof in itself that he lived on the least and was never lured by luxury. He preferred austerity and was never attached to body or its ever-growing demands.

Half-naked: This signifies the fact that he belonged to the tradition of the *rishis*; he did not exactly wear a *kaupin* (a small piece of cloth wore around the waist to cover private parts) as a declaration that he had not renunciated the world, to teach that it was better to live on little than to indulge in misdeeds.

Barefooted: He chose to be barefooted so that he could feel the soil, could be free from fear as there was no danger on the earth; be in constant touch with the mother earth and feel the hard realities of life.

***Khuli Shikha*:** *Shikha* is the unbound lock of hair on the crown left after tonsure of head. It was left loose for a particular purpose. It reminded him of his vow, kept him conscious and dedicated towards the ideal, the goal, the purpose, and gave meaning and direction to his life and actions.

A Book in Hand: He carried wisdom, which is a Brahmin's only wealth.

Fearlessness: Again, it is a Brahmin's greatest possession. He was fearless because of his inner strength of knowledge, inherent purity, confidence and determination not to do anything wrong or for selfish or personal gain.

In this way, Chanakya has become a symbol that has sustained itself as an ideal for around twenty-five centuries. His image has been created by people down the ages after studying his writings and following his dictums. There is no authentic painting or statue to validate it. Though, it is well-supported by his ideas, ideals and actions known.

It can be easily surmised that the scholars and historians must have studied and analysed every bit of scriptures, literature, philosophy, politics, economics, law, medicine, warfare and all the sixteen (often eighteen) disciplines taught at that time in Taxila and other Universities of India to know more about Chanakya and his times. After completing his education from Taxila, Chanakya became a teacher there. It is mentioned in history that as a teacher he worked as an informer to the King, with his students as spies.

He always had diverse things in mind and pursued different goals at a time.

The popularity of Chanakya as well as the significance of his teachings can be gauged by the fact that at least in India whosoever shows some wisdom is called Chanakya and given the nickname 'Chanak'. It is because he was a man balanced of ideas and action. Chanakya was a theoretician and a pragmatic philosopher who presented his theories according to the ideals and the ideals in accordance with the theories. His ideas and actions balanced each other. He honestly expressed them. If he thought that the end justified the means then he boldly declared it. He did not hide anything and never kept anyone in the dark. An enemy was an enemy; friendship with him could be developed only to ruin him. He believed that even forgiveness must serve some definite purpose; it should not be meaningless and must bring good results and gain.

Chanakya was very fond of his parents. He was disciplined and obedient, although he was their only child. He lost them before he left Taxila after learning all the sixteen *shastras*. There is no proof that he ever got married.

Childhood and Education

Chanakya was a man of great courage. He worshipped knowledge. He advocated learning and tried his best to show the importance of proper education. He courageously and openly declared the parents who fail to educate their children to be their enemies:

Mātā shatru pitā bairi yena balo nā pāthitah

There was little known about him till he reached the court of the Magadh Naresh Dhananand who laughed at his ugliness. That insult was too much for a young learned

Brahmin who was full of wisdom and spirit, and did not approve of the luxurious and idle living of the King and his courtiers at the cost of public security and welfare, and also the atrocities inflicted by them on the general public. The result was the same which could be expected from a sublime pandit — '*nripasya vināsham*'.

In the court, in the presence of all, he loosened the lock on his crown and took a vow to destroy the king and his dynasty completely. His fame spread out from there, from the court to the outside world, among the people. His popularilty grew when he started making incessant attacks on the King, kept him needlessly busy and restless. His final success made him known to all. With the demolition of the Nand Dynasty and the inception of Maurya Dynasty, he became popular and respectable. The new laws and reliefs, the organisation, the way of management and justice enhanced his reputation and respect, which immediately and earnestly changed into adoration and worship. The treaty with Alexander carried his fame to distant land and when he wrote down his political and economic theories and the moral and ethical treatises, he became immortal. He still enjoys that immortal status.

Chanakya did so much during his short lifespan that it is difficult to point out which of his achievements is greater than the other. One of his greatest achievements was his idea of a unified India and his success in binding the whole country and bringing it under one *Chakravarti Samrat*. When the whole country was divided into numerous small kingdoms, he dreamed of unity and security of all the kingdoms. Of course, the idea must have come after the attack of Alexander. He made Chandragupta Maurya the emperor of India in about 325 BC. Then he destroyed the power of his opponents and eliminated them through well-planned administrative schemes. By keeping Chandragupta Maurya in the lead, he expanded the empire to the borders of Persia, beyond the barriers of the Vindhya Range to the south, making it a vast and the most extensive empire in the history of ancient India. The empire ranged from the Himalayas and the Kabul valley in modern Afghanistan to the southern tip of India. Though he did not take the credit for the same, but it was possible only because of an excellent administration that he planned, executed and later on penned down in his famous treatise *Artha Shastra*. He laid the foundation of a strong India, which was not invaded for many centuries till it remained united. But after Harshvardhan, it was again divided and numerous small and sovereign kingdoms came up, which prompted and invited the invaders for a series of attacks, which turned India into a slave country and it remained under foreign rule for more than one thousand years.

Chanakya, the seer, who could foresee the future, with the sheer power of his character, achieved unachievable height, unified a divided and tattered country and showed the world numerous ways to achieve one's target. He lived his life overworking in pursuit of his dreams and visions and died 'the death of old age' some time in 275 BC to live for ever as an epitome of wisdom, confidence, determination and success.

His life was all work and least rest. It was not a struggle for personal existence (he was always in danger, but never felt it). It was a growing struggle for the welfare of the people and peace and security for the country.

Chanakya is said to be the greatest statesman, strategist and politician, but most of the people forget that throughout his life he remained basically a disciplined and dedicated student, a wise and commanding teacher and a prolific and honest writer. The one great quality in him, which usually remains undetected and undiscussed, is that he tested each and every thing before teaching or writing.

He led a well-lived, well-utilised and sublime life in a mundane and conspiring world, which had little humanity left. That humanity was grabbed, eaten up and finished by humans, and people were living in an inhuman world cruelly dominated by man. Chanakya is immortal. More so because he neither allowed Chandragupta to be a dictator nor he himself got the pride from the triumphs, status, power and respect that he got. He truly remained a true, pure and sublime Brahmin till the end; so time failed to obliterate him.

The whole world is indebted to him for almost all the scholars have drawn from his teachings directly from his books or indirectly from the laws based on the concepts given by him, but adopted by another country. They work as a base for many theories and hypotheses.

The Varied Writings of Chanakya

In his writings, he is not just 'Chanakya' but many writers combined and absorbed in one. His childhood name was Vishnu Gupta, which is similar to Vishnu Sharma who wrote *Hitopadesh*, so he is claimed to be the same. He was the son of Chanak, so he was called Chanakya and wrote all the moral teachings including *Chanakya Niti* and *Chanakya Sutra* under this name. Kautilya who wrote *Artha Shastra* is said to be Chanakya himself and as Vatsyayan, he gave the really astonishing work *Kamasutra*.

The science of ethics (*Niti Shastra*) or moral teaching in Indian scriptures has its own value and significance. Its importance can be gauged by the fact that in *The Gita* Lord Krishna declared, "I'm ethics for those who wish to win" — *nitih asmi jigistām*.

From the Vedic Period till 1200 AD, the science of ethics remained as a mode and form of expression, and the sharpest device to teach. The Vedas, Brahma, Vishnu, Shiva, Ram, Krishna, Vyas, Brihaspati, Shukra, Indra, Markandeya, Bharadwaj, Vaishampayan, Buddha, Mahavira, Chanakya,

Bhartrihari, Nanak, Kabir, Tulasi, Rahim and many more through their scriptures have added something valuable to the science of ethics and enriched it.

In Sanskrit, there are many books which deal purely with pure moral teachings both in the form of couplet (generally *anushtupa* metre) and also as simple formula known as *sutra*. In them, the thinkers have presented ways to purify our inner selves and have taught to get success in every situation and circumstance, and lead a peaceful and happy life. They have discussed these ideas using various similes and metaphors, which makes them impressive and have a magical effect on the listeners. In almost every congregation (in *panchayats* for any reason, and at the time of important sales and purchases), they are quoted vehemently and analysed methodically. They are often quoted to impress others. Clarity and easy perception are their qualities that are behind their miraculously long life and popularity. They are so natural that they touch the heart and so true that none can deny them. They will not perish till man is alive.

Chanakya is a leader among all the writers who wrote Indian scriptures. He has not narrated the events, but has given the conclusions. He has not described anything in detail, he has just squeezed and condensed them to suit his direct and concise ways of expression.

He was a great statesman, diplomat, and a sagacious and virtuous man in moral behaviour. He has a special place among the composers of ethical verses, for he dedicated all his writings solely to moral teachings and composed nothing else other than that. He had an aim, which he achieved. He excelled in every sphere. He was truly a committed soul. Such commitment has never been seen after his departure. It is no wonder that he was read, quoted, liked and revered by all. His teachings are universal and applicable at every place and in any situation. Just by following him, one can easily get worldly success in any field and also spiritual solace.

Chanakya framed policies with rare prudence, clarity and judiciousness. They are still treated as the basis of diplomacy and formation of policies and rules by most of the governments of the world. He is the most popular and the most widely read person among the ancient Indian writers.

Most of the moral and ethical quotes are associated with the name of Chanakya. As we know virtually nothing about the poets and thinkers, so we have no option but to accept them as they are placed before us. We have no extra information to challenge any part of it, though we find the same couplet and the same doctrine at many places, even in the classics that are supposed to have been written centuries before Chanakya; as for example many of them are included in *Manu Smriti*, *Mahabharat* and Puranas.

The following *shloka* is found in Chanakya's *Niti Shastra*, *Hitopadesha* as well as in *Markandeya Purana* (37/23), in *Varaha Purana* (153/26) and in the *Shanti Parva* of *Mahabharat*:

Nāsti vidyāsamam chakshuh nāsti satyasamam tapah

Nāsti rāgsamam dukham nāsti tyāgsamam sukham

Most of them are called *Chanakya Niti* and *Chanakya Sutra*. In Vishwesharanand Indological Series No. 27, 28 and 29 (published in 1963 from Hoshiarpur) such six versions have been collected:

1. **Vriddha Chanakya (Part I)** — It is known as *Samanya Vachana* (General Version). It has 8 chapters.

2. **Vriddha Chanakya (Part II)** — It is known as *Alankrita Vachana* (Ornamental Version). It is named as *Chanakya Nitidarpan* and has 17 chapters, which have 197 *shlokas* out of the total available 336. In the easily available versions in the market, all the 336 *shlokas* have been included and they are called either *Chanakya Nitidarpan* or *Chanakya Niti Shastra.*

3. **Chanakya Niti Shastra** — It is the third version and is called *Chanakya Niti Shastra.* In the *Avatarnika* (Preface), it has been claimed that it has been collected from different books and it is the seed of all scriptures:

   Nānāshāstra udhritam wakhshye rājnitisammuchayam

   Srababeejam idam shāshtam Chānakyam sārsangraham

It has been claimed to be the original work of Chanakya, which is a proof that it is the most ancient one:

Mulasutram prawakshyāmi Chānakyena yathoditam

Yasya vigyānamātrena murkho bhawati panditah

4. **Chanakya Sarsangrah** — It is the fourth version, which contains 300 *Anushtupa Britta Tis* divided into three sections and each section contains exactly 100 *shlokas*. It teaches not only polity, but also the simple ways of general living. The last couplet lays stress on 'living in Kashi' which shows the love of the poet for the place and suggests that either he belonged to Kashi or had great affinity and respect for the place. So he tells 'in this mortal world, there are four things which can be of essence; they are living in Kashi, truthful living, closeness to Ganga and devotion to Lord Shiva':

Asāre khalu samsāre sārametat chatushtayam
Kāshyām bāsah satām sango Gangāmbhah
Shambhusevanam

5. **Laghu Chanakya** — It is divided into 8 chapters and each contains 10 to 13 couplets. It was not available in India but was very popular in European countries for many centuries as it was carried over there by the priests. Perhaps it was first translated in Greek in the year 1825 by Gelenas who was probably a scholar of Sanskrit.

6. **Chanakya Rajniti Shastra** — It is divided into 8 chapters and contains 534 *shlokas* or couplets in Sanskrit. Even this book was not available in India. It was translated in the 9th century AD and preserved in Tibet. Its verses are also available in the books in China, Mangolia, Manchuria, Java and Bali. But the complete text is available only in Tibet.

Chanakya Rajniti Shastra deals mostly with kings and politics; particularly the fourth and the fifth chapters deal only with the king, kingdom, people, policies, diplomacy and other topics related to good and successful governance. In this respect, it is a unique creation which teaches everyone all about emancipation of life, good moral character, happy, smooth and trouble-free life, good governance and the duties of kings, ministers and other government official, so that they can rule well and protect the kingdom from inner revolts and outer attacks. Even Brihaspati in his *Niti Shastra* has included verses from Chanakya's *Rajniti Shastra*. It is claimed that originally it contained some 1119 *shlokas*. In that way, it appears that the total number of the *shlokas* composed by Chanakya is more than two thousand.

To many, *Niti shlokas* have greater value but for many, Kautilya's *Artha Shastra* is the greatest work. Incidentally, Kautilya means crookedness, cunningness and fraud; somehow these qualities got associated with Chanakya although he was totally against them and despised these impurities. In *Mudra Rakshasa*, he has been introduced as:

Kautilyah kutilmatih sa yesha yena krodhāgnnau

prasamadāhi Nandbanshah

— *Mudra Rakshasa* (1/7)

Politics, kingship, governance and economy are all related aspects of life. They do not have separate existence. They are interrelated and interdependent. In the *Artha Shastra*, Chanakya has comprehensively discussed, theorised and presented every aspect of the ruler's life as well as that of the ruled. The principles have abundance of practical wisdom and humanitarian idealism. It deliberately and with great success combines them with strict rules, tough aims to balance the socio-economic and political scenario and its transformation into action, and implementation in day-to-day life for maximum gain, peaceful and trouble-free life. That attitude is well supported by tradition as it assimilates tradition and by human psychology, both general and abnormal. They have been presented in such a way that they need no proof. Subsidiary materials are not needed to substantiate them.

Chanakya Sutras are mostly taken from Kautilya's *Artha Shastra*. They present the quintessence of Chanakya's views and those of the earlier texts, particularly from *Brihaspati Niti*. On the contrary to the present belief and effort to separate politics and religion, Chanakya held the view that they are inseparable.

Nyaya Shastra Mimamsa, a commentary on jurisprudence and *Kamasutra* by Vatsyayan are also supposed to be the creations of Chanakya. The information can neither be ignored easily nor accepted whole-heartedly. There is one vital fact that Vatsyayan is believed to be a person of the age and the court of Kanishka. In absence of adequate proof, it depends entirely on the mood and mind of an individual to accept or to deny it. It makes no difference to the wisdom and greatness of Chanakya.

It is a surprise that he wrote *Kamasutra* under the name of Vatsyayan. It is a book which deals with sex and physical relation between a man and a woman. The very subject may have forced him to change his name. This work is basically a treatise that describes various ways and procedures by which carnal pleasure can be achieved.

Panchatantra, including *Hitopadesh* and *Mitralabh*, is also accepted as the work of Chanakya as he is accepted as Vishnu Gupta or Vishnu Sharma. However, some of the scholars feel that they are different persons born in different ages. Chanakya is also known by the name Vishnu Gupta and seldom Vishnu Sharma. *Panchatantra*, as is known to all, is composed by Vishnu Sharma. Yet, it is not only the similarity of name, but also a few *shlokas* which have been found common in it and in the books popularly known as the writings of Chanakya. There is no debate possible on this issue. When most of his works came back to India from the possession of different countries, then how can anyone be sure of the text or the author?

It may seem debatable who composed these *shlokas* and when they were composed, but there is no doubt that these are the jewels of human mind and the most precious possessions for the present, which should be preserved well for the future generations. People from all walks of life, whether literate or illiterate, must know and follow them for a better understanding of people and life. If sincerely followed, it will check everything wrong, improve the standard of thinking and general behaviour, which will automatically help in living a satisfied and peaceful life, not with plenty of money but with a lot of achievements.

In all that Chanakya wrote his intentions were very clear. He wanted to improve general moral character, create an ideal society and to show the people the ways to lead a contented, peaceful and happy life. He never thought about himself and accumulated no wealth. He did everything for the people.

Leaves from the Life of Chanakya

His Childhood

One famous incident from his childhood proves him to belong to Magadh in closer vicinity to Patliputra.

One day a kush (a kind of grass, with a sharp needle-like top, used in the religious observances by the Hindus) pricked in the foot of Chanak, the father of Chanakya. It became a septic and eventually Chanak died. Chanakya did observe the rituals but he could neither forget nor forgive kush. He studied it, made preparations and started uprooting and annihilating the very species of kush by pouring whey at the broken roots of kush so that they may not germinate or grow again. It was his way of showing anger and taking vengeance.

The people were amazed to see it. A young man taking whey every morning and going out in search of *kush* uprooting them and pouring at each root a bit of whey to erase them was a sight to watch. Some of them did not like it. They protested. It had no effect on the mind and action of the revengeful and determined Chanakya. One day, some elderly persons went to Chanakya who was busy in uprooting and destroying quite innocent looking but sharp needle-like *kush*. They politely asked, "What are you doing and why?"

"I'm uprooting and destroying this pinching *kush* because I can't tolerate anything against man or humanity, and whosoever goes against man or humanity I'll destroy that like it," he replied.

He was true to his words, never neutral. He usually took a balanced side and often extreme steps. He would not easily express his mind, for he held the view that one should not make his inner decisions known to others. He said:

Manasā vichintyayet vachasā nā prakāshayet

At some places, it is written that once he was going to some place with his disciples. He had taken less treaded route. He wore no protection for his feet. A *kush* pricked him. It was painful. He immediately asked the pupils to bring whey, uproot the *kush* and pour whey in each root to abolish it completely. When other men asked him the reason of his anger, he plainly replied that he could not tolerate any obstacle in his way.

The Vow

There are different versions of each incident associated with Chanakya. This one is not an exception. Usually, it is said that Chanakya went to the court of Magadh Naresh Dhananand on his own but another version says that because he was a scholar, he was made the president of a charity trust and met the king for the first time as the president of the said trust. But it cannot be true, for all such appointments were made directly by the king. There is yet another version that one minister from the court of the Magadh Naresh who was angry with him as he was insulted by the king, took Chanakya to the court. He knew something about the background, power and nature of Chanakya. He invited him to the court knowing fully well that the king will not tolerate his black face and arrogant ways. He will insult the Brahmin and the Brahmin will take the revenge. Thus, his aim will be fulfilled. He did exactly as he planned and truly enough the egoistic king forgot the courtesy to be shown towards a Brahmin. He laughed at the black and ugly Brahmin and said, "A Brahmin can't be black and if black he can't be a Brahmin." It had dual meanings.

Chanakya protested but of no avail. The minister concerned was pleased with the expected turn in the event. He sided with his king and poured *ghee* in already rising flames. The situation grew tense. Many of them did not like an insult to a Brahmin, but Dhananand was obstinate. He would not listen to reason. He loved luxury and was cruel to the people. He had brutally taxed the people to fill the royal treasury. People were annoyed. He was not liked by them.

Dhananand started laughing at the Brahmin who was fast losing his patience. He roared against the king in the court. In return the king ordered, "Throw this Brahmin out of the court." It brought the end of his preserved patience. Chanakya broke loose. He showered verbal curses on the king and his kingdom. No one was able to subdue him. In a fit of anger, Dhananand inflicted more injury. The angry Brahmin freed himself from the grip of the soldiers, untied the sacred lock of hair at his crown and tock a vow, "Dhananand, I had come to show you the true path and stop you from luxurious living, free you from *sura* and *sundari* (wine and women) but you won't listen to reason.

I take a vow in the presence of all that I will annihilate you and your dynasty. I won't take rest till you are destroyed along with your posterity." He marched out of the court in that angry mood.

The king was not worried as to what a feeble Brahmin could do to him but Chanakya was restless. He had taken a great vow. It was obviously very difficult to fulfil. He lost his appetite. He stopped thinking about anything else. He had only the Nand Dynasty in his mind. It took a lot of time, but finally he succeeded in completely destroying the Magadh Naresh and his Nand Dynasty.

A Boy's Judgement

Chanakya was a learned man, a practical thinker, a proud Brahmin, a conscious executive and an immaculate planner. He had taken the vow to destroy the Nand Dynasty completely. His loosened long and thick central lock behind his head always reminded him that the vow is still to be fulfilled. He chalked out the plan to generate resources and raise an army to do the needful. He knew that he was not a warrior, that he was able to carry the books but not the sword, and that he was a strategist but not a killer. He could lead an army from behind but could not move in the front. He needed a brave soldier, a lenient man, a disciplined disciple, a wise, strong and handsome youth, and a person who could mix with ball without losing his individual status. He knew only such a person could fulfil his dreams, execute his plans, change his ideas into reality and ascend the peak.

One day in the plains of Ganga in a rich looking village full of greenery, he saw cows and cowboys. He was attracted by a tall boy who held his head high and was standing on a big stone. He was looking at the cattle and directing the boys. He was posing to be the king. Chanakya was engrossed in the drama. The boy sat on the stone as if it were a throne. He sent many boys as messengers and soldiers to do the tit-bits. He saw the black Brahmin, called him and when Chanakya approached him, he asked, "What do you want, learned Brahmin?" The boy knew how to honour a Brahmin.

Chanakya humbly replied, "I need cows to feed my pupils."

The boy knew the value of charity. Without any hesitation he ordered, "This learned Brahmin should be given one hundred one cows."

Chanakya bowed humbly and asked, "Have you taken permission from your guardians?"

"A king does not need to take permission from others." The boy knew the powers of a king and was sure that he was doing something good. One must be charitable.

In the same mood, Chanakya asked, "Where are your parents?"

The boy directed his index finger towards the village. Chanakya then read his forehead and also got an opportunity to read his palm. He saw what he wished to see. He started listening to the boy more intently. The boy said, "I've no father. My mother lives there."

"And what's the name of your mother?" Chanakya wanted to know more.

"Mata Mura" was the reply.

"Victory to the king! I will come back to take the cows," Chanakya blessed the boy and turned towards the village. He met his mother expressed his wish to take the boy so that he could make him a king. She was not willing to part with the only child that she had. The boy was on the mother's side. Chanakya spent the whole evening and the whole night in convincing them. The next morning was a bright one. Finally, Chanakya was able to take the boy to Taxila to educate and train him.

The boy was baptised. He was given a new name 'Chandragupta' to which the name of his mother Mura was added as Maurya. Chanakya made him the king, Chandragupta Maurya, and started the Mauryan Dynasty, one of the greatest dynasties in the ancient Indian History and a period that is still taken as the golden period.

The village was Pippali Kanan full of mango orchards in the Champakaranya. It was here where Rama stayed for two days while returning from Janakpur after the marriage with Sita. A pond was dug there which is known as 'Sita Kunda'. The mango grove is still there and there are two small temples – Shiva Temple and Rama Temple. It is some one hundred twenty kilometres from Patliputra in the north. After becoming the minister and establishing the Mauryan Dynasty, Chanakya started living there. He had a special fascination for the place.

A Practical Suggestion

In three different ways and occasions, Chanakya attacked Magadh under the leadership of Chandragupta and every time he was defeated. He was desolate. He was unable to pinpoint the mistake. The worried Chanakya was mentally taxed and paying heavy interest.

Customarily, he would loiter during the night to take stock of the situation and to keep an eye over the happenings. One late night when he was passing through a village, he saw light coming out from a hut. He automatically turned towards it. There were many small holes in the hut and it was easy to see all that was happening inside.

From the conversation going inside, Chanakya gathered that the hut belonged to a widow. She had a son. She had brought some grain late in the evening. She had laboured hard for hours to be able to cook a meal.

When the boy started eating, he tried to take a morsel from the middle and in the process burnt his fingers. (In another version, he took a bite from the middle of bread.) In either case, the mother was angry.

"You fool!" she said, "You're behaving like Chanakya. Food is never eaten from the centre. It is always eaten from the side."

Chanakya heard it and was highly amazed, as the practical suggestion was like a boon to him. He thought over it for a long time, realised his mistake and returned back satisfied and confident. It is needless to state that from there on, he started attacking the kingdoms at the outskirts. Dhananand was not able to send his army in time and started losing trying to control and protect the centre. Chandragupta won every such smaller kingdom. There was no dearth of wealth and army. Enriched by such small victories, Chanakya gave the final blow and won the biggest and richest kingdom of Magadh. He felt satiated, now that his vow was fulfilled.

Saved the King from Poison

In the absence of a vigilant guardian like Chanakya it would have been rather impossible for Chandragupta to survive, for by winning different territories he was winning friends as well as making enemies. It was the age of poison girls (*vish kanyas*) who were trained in different ways to administer poison to selected persons, mostly kings, princes and rich young men. They were made to take poison every day through snake bites or directly in the form of powder or tablet. This made them poisonous and poisoned their system and organs so that the person who made relations with them was killed. On the other hand, they also kept different types of poisons hidden in their apparel and were trained to administer enough out of the secretly kept poison to wipe out the target.

One such poison girl was planted to kill Chandragupta Maurya. She came to the court with a secret agent. They offered many things to the king. Their first aim was to gain the favour of the king without making Chanakya suspicious. It was a well thought out and dexterously executed plan. They came very close to the king. They would come to the court every day and return back before the evening.

As they were expecting, one day Chandragupta made the crucial and deadly mistake of inviting them to dinner. In the late evening, they came again for the dinner. The poison girl had everyone present there in view including the service men coming in and going out. She mixed the poison. The moment it was done, Chanakya appeared and ordered the soldiers to arrest them. He had kept them under surveillance and was watchful. When the invitation was extended to them he intuitively knew what was to happen, so he had made all arrangements to avoid the worst and to get them arrested along with the proof.

Though an obedient disciple, yet Chandragupta did not like the interference of his guru and minister. But he became dumbfounded to see the overwhelming proof. At his heart, he was thankful to his mentor and guide for making him what he was and for saving him.

The Appointment of the Minister-in-chief

Nand Dynasty was finished. Maurya Dynasty had taken a grand and bright start. Chandragupta Maurya ascended the throne. The job of unifying the nation was almost over. Peace and normalcy was restored in the kingdom. Chanakya wanted to see everything secure. Though he was efficiently looking after everything, he was also feeling badly the need of a Prime Minister. He was looking for one.

One man from the enemy camp had impressed him as wise, sincere, honest and truthful to the king. He was the famous, rather notorious Amatya Rakshasa, who had earnt the nickname of Rakshasa, because of his tough stands and very severe punishments. One thing in him that Chanakya appreciated most was the fact that Amatya did not desert the losing king. He remained true to him and fought for him tooth and nail till the end. He decided to make him the Prime Minister to serve the Mauryan Empire.

On the other hand, Amatya Rakshasa did not like Chanakya. He hated him for ruining the king that he was faithful to. Chanakya met him and asked him to be the Prime Minister. Amatya Rakshasa blatantly refused.

Intermittently, he kept on persuading him to accept the post and to serve the new empire. He used various means to entice the rigid Amatya, who had his prejudices against Chanakya and was unable to shake them off.

After a few days, his secret agents brought some news. Amatya was to attend a function at the residence of a businessman at the most crowded intersection. Chanakya reached there earlier and stopped him. He openly invited him there to become the Prime Minister. He told, "A Prime Minister is not responsible to a king or to a government or to the board of ministers, he is responsible to the land and the people. The people have a right to see the best person at that high pedestal. You have the ability. People have faith in you. You must accept this challenging job."

Though it might seem to be a desperate attempt on the part of Chanakya but it was a calculated step. Amatya Rakshasa was in a fix. He was trapped. After a lot of discussions, he accepted the post. It is a rare example when the right hand man of the defeated king was made the Prime Minister.

There is a very famous play entitled *Mudra Rakshasa* in Sanskrit that deals with this as a central subject.

Chandragupta's Marriage with Helen

Chanakya thought of the welfare of the nation. India was passing through a critical phase. It was a period of transition. He wanted the security of the country and safety to its people. Greeks were still there. Alexander had returned back. He had appointed Seleucus Nicator to govern India. Chanakya was looking out a way to make him friend and grab the kingdom which was still under his control. He knew well about his daughter Helen, also known as Cornelia. He planned the marriage of Chandragupta with Helen.

He announced his decision to his dear pupil and king. Chandragupta was in a fix. He was not in a position to deny his mentor but he secretly loved a girl named Chitra. He wanted to marry her. He was looking for an opportune moment to declare his intention. Chanakya knew everything.

He had planned everything. He had to consolidate the position. Chandragupta got the opportunity and declared his love and willingness to marry Chitra. Chanakya was not lenient. He did not listen to the king and forced him to marry Cornelia. The king had to surrender to his guru.

In all probability, the marriage was solemnised in 305 BC, when Seleucus Nicator was defeated in the battle. As dowry and as defeated general, he gave four big provinces to Chanakya. They were Kabul, Kandhar, Herat and Makaran. The details of this war are available in *Indica* written by Megasthenes.

It is also claimed that later on Chandragupta married Chitra. This theme has been dramatically and poetically given the form of a play entitled *Chandragupta* by Jaishankar Prasad, a famous poet and dramatist of Hindi.

The Lamp

This incident has perhaps been described by Megasthenes in *Indica*. It is related to him. He had come to India and had heard about Chanakya. He wanted to meet him. It was not difficult to meet him. He sent words and was allowed to go to the hut in which Chanakya was living.

When Megasthenes reached there, it was the first hour of the evening. Chanakya was writing something under the dim light of an earthen lamp. He raised his head, welcomed the guest and asked, "What's your purpose?"

"I've come to see you and talk to you about yourself and on different topics." So was the candid reply of the foreigner.

Chanakya asked him to wait. Then he took another lamp and after lighting it, he put off the first lamp. Then he invited Megasthenes to sit on the broad mat. Megasthenes sat down but could not hide his surprise. He asked, "I feel there must be a reason that you have put off the first lamp and lighted another one, but I don't find any difference in them; neither in the make and size nor the light that is coming out. Please tell me why you changed the lamp."

"Before changing it, I asked about your purpose. I came to know that it is a personal meeting. So I put off the official lamp whose oil comes from the government treasury and I lighted the lamp for which I purchase oil from my salary. While doing a personal work, I can't misuse the government's money." Chanakya gave a simple reply.

It was really unbelievable for the visitor. He knew Chanakya was all powerful in the Mauryan kingdom, yet he was behaving in such an honest way. He bowed before him and said, "This is the reason of ycur immense power."

The Active Retirement

After taking voluntary retirement, he wrote great works and penned down his experiences in exquisite form. That way he immortalised his wisdom for the posterity to use. On the one hand, he wrote freely, and on the other, he kept sharp and agile eyes on the social and political functioning and developments of the nation that he had built up, and on his dear pupil for the sake of the dearest motherland.

It is evident from what is available that Chanakya had intensely sharp and observant eyes along with a correlating and synthesising mind, which left nothing out of view and away from meaningful consideration. He had the opportunity to learn and see the turmoil, suffering, pain, luxury, loot, injustice, invasions, corruptions and everything else that was happening in the closer vicinity and at a fair distance. Most of the time, he was himself in the firing line. He had accumulated an overflowing wealth of knowledge. He knew that as a minister he could serve the living people but he would not be able to share his wealth. He decided to bring out that treasure and store in books for the posterity. For that he needed enough time, suitable and peaceful place and constant flow of current information. So, he made all the necessary arrangements and announced his voluntary retirement after appointing Amatya Rakshasa as the Prime Minister. All were shocked at it including the new Amatya who was expecting incessant interference from him.

None of them agreed to the proposal but it was Chanakya who was known for taking concrete decisions after a great deal of thinking over weighing all the pros and cons. He succeeded in subsiding the temporary furore and retired for deep meditation and useful writing.

He happily and wisely spent his last days in active retirement.

SECTION – II

Chanakya Niti

Niti - 1

1. ॐ

Pranamya shirsā Vishnum trailokyādhipatim prabhum

Nānāshāstroddhritam wakshye rājnitisamuchayam

After humbly bowing down to the Emperor of the three worlds (the earth, heaven and hell), the Almighty Lord Vishnu, I herewith present the maxims of the science of political ethics, *Rajniti Shastra*, selected from different treatises/scriptures.

2. ॐ

Adhityedam yathāshāstram naro jānāti sattamah

Dharmopadeshbikhyātam kāryākāryam subhāsubham

By studying these maxims taken from the *shastras*, one acquires knowledge of the best principles to be followed in life and understands what ought or what ought not to be done, what is good or bad, religious or irreligious, sin or virtue.

3. ॐ

Tadaham sampravakshyāmi lokānām hitakāmyayā
Yen vugyānmātrena sarbagyatwam prapadyate

Therefore with an eye to the public good, I am presenting the knowledge, which will lead to the correct understanding of things in their proper perspective, if and when learnt well.

4. ॐ

Murkhashishyopadeshena dushtastribharanena cha
Dukhitaih samprayogena panditoapyawasidati

Even a wise man comes to grief and feels depression if he imparts instructions to a foolish disciple or when maintains a wicked wife or when comes in close contact with the miserable.

5. ॐ

Dushṭā bhāryā shatham mitram bhrityaschotardāyaka
Sasarpe cha griheābaso mriturewa nā sanshayah

A wicked wife, a foolish friend, an ill-tongued servant and living in a house infested with serpents will undoubtedly bring death.

6. ॐ

Āpadarthe dhanam raksheda dārānraksheda dhanairapi
Ātmānam satatam raksheda dārairapi dhanarapi

One should save his money against hard times, save his wife against spending or sacrificing the money and one should save 'self' even at the cost of the wife and the riches.

7. ॐ

Āpadarthe dhanam raksheda srimatam kuta āpadah
Kadāchida chalitā Lakshmih sanchitoapi vinashayati

Save your wealth against unforeseen calamities without thinking that a rich man has no fear of a calamity. Wealth has supple legs. Even saved riches are destroyed.

8. ॐ

Yasmindeshe nā sammāno nā vitirna cha vāndhawah
Nā cha vidyā āgamah kaschit tam desham parivarjayeta

One should not inhabit a country where one gets no respect, no opportunity to earn one's livelihood, where one has no friends or relatives, or from where one cannot acquire knowledge.

9. ॐ

Dhanikah shrotriyo rājā nadi vaidyastu panchamah
Panch yatra nā vidyate nā tatra diwasam vaseta

Do not stay there even for a single day where there is no rich man, no king, no learned Brahmin, no river or no doctor.

10. ॐ

Lokayātrā bhayam lajja dākshinatyam tyagsheelata
Panch yatra nā vidyante nā kuryāt tatra sansthitim

One should never live there where there are no means of earning one's livelihood, where the people have no dread of anybody, have no sense of shame, no intelligence, nor a charitable nature.

11. ॐ

Jāniyāt preshne bhrityān bāndhawānvyasanā agame
Mitram cha āpatti kaleshu bhāryām cha bibhava chhaye

Test a servant while he is on his duty and a relative in difficulty, test a friend in adversity, and a wife in misfortune.

12. ॐ

Āture vyasane prāpte durbhikshe shatru-sankate
Rājdwāre smasāne cha yah tisthati sa bāndhawa

He is a true friend and sincere relative who cooperates and stands by in time of need, depression, misfortune, famine, a war, in a king's court, or at the crematorium (the place of last rituals where the dead are put on a pyre).

13. ॐ

Yo dhruvāni parityajya adhruvam parishevte
Dhruvāni tasya nashyanti adhruvam nashtamev cha

He who opts up for an uncertain thing leaving behind the certain things, loses that which is in possession and fails to get what is already perishable.

14. ॐ

Varyeta kuljā prāgyo virupāmpi kanyakām
Rupwatim nā nichasya vivāhah sadrise kule

Wise man should marry a virgin of a respectable family even if she is deformed. He should not marry one of a low-class family, though beautiful. Marriage in a family of equal status is preferable.

15. ॐ

Nakhinām cha nadinām cha shringinām shastra pāninām

Viswāso naiva kartavya strisu rājkuleshu cha

Do not put trust in rivers, in men who carry weapons, wild animals with claws or horns, in women, and in the members of a royal family.

16. ॐ

Vishādapyamritam grāhyamamedhyādapi kānchanam

Nichādpyuttamā vidyā striratnam duskulādapi

If there is nectar in poison, it should be extracted; if gold has fallen in filth it should be taken out, washed and kept; if a low-born person possesses knowledge, he should be treated respectfully; in the same way a girl born in the family of evil-doers be accepted, if she possesses virtuous qualities.

17. ॐ

Strinām dwiguna āhāro buddhistāsām chaturgunā

Sāhasam shadgunam chaiva kāmoastaguna uchchayate

Women eat double than men, they have four times more wisdom than men, they have six times more courage, and eight times more sensual urge than men.

Niti – 2

1. ॐ

Anritam sāhasam māyā murkhatwam ati lubadhatā

Ashouchatwam nirdayatwam strinām doshah swabhāvajā

Untruthfulness, rashness, guile, stupidity, avarice, unseemliness and cruelty are a woman's seven natural flaws.

2. ॐ

Bhojya bhojanshaktischa ratishaktirvarānganā

Bibhavo dānshaktischa nā alpasya tapasah phalam

It is a great boon of extraordinary austerities to get healthy and delicious dishes, to eat them and to have a strong system to digest them, to have a beautiful socially accepted wife and to be virile in her company, and to have a longing and mental setup for charity in prosperity. All these are boons.

3. ॐ

Asya putro bashibhuto bhāryā chhandā anugāmini

Bibhawe yashcha santustastasya swarga ehaiwa hi

He has his heaven here on the earth whose son is obedient, whose wife follows his wishes and who is content with what he has.

4. ॐ

Te putrā ye piturbhaktāh sa pitā yastu poshakah

Tanmitram yasya viswāsah sā bhāryā yatra nirbritih

They alone can be called sons who are devoted to their fathers. Only he is a father who fosters, feeds and supports his sons. Only he is a friend who is faithful and only she is a wife who gives peace and keeps contented.

5. ॐ

Parokshe kāryahantāram pratyakshe priyavadinam

Varjayetādrisham mitram bishkumbham payomukham

Break all your relations with such a friend who talks sweetly in your presence but brings harm at your back. Such a person is like a pitcher of poison with milk on top.

6. ॐ

Nā viswaset kumitre cha mitre chā api nā viswaset

Kadāchit kupitam mitram sarba guhyam prakāshyet

Do not put all your trust in a false friend or even a close friend, for if he gets angry he will reveal all your secrets.

7. ॐ

Manasā chintitam kāryam vāchā nā prakāshyet

Mantrena rakshayed gudham kārye chā api niyojayet

Do not reveal what you have planned to do, the best counsel is to keep it secret and try to execute it with determination.

8. ॐ

Kashtam cha khalu murkhatwam cha khalu yauvanam

Kashtātookashtataram chaiva pargehaniwasanam

Foolishness is painful and the youth too is painful, but more painful by far than either is to take shelter in another person's house.

9. ॐ

Shaile shaile nā mānikyam mauktikam nā gaje gaje

Sādhawo nā hi sarbatra chandanam nā vane vane

There is no gem in every mountain, and no pearl in the head of every elephant; similarly saints are not found everywhere and sandalwood trees are not seen in every forest.

10. ॐ

Putrāshcha vividhaih sheelairniyojyāh satatam budhaih

Nitigyah sheelsampannā bhawanti kulpujitāh

Wise men should bring up their sons carefully in various moral ways, for only those bring glory to family-tradition who are well-behaved and well-versed in moral and ethical knowledge.

11. ॐ

Mātā shatruh pitā vairi yen bāl nā pāthitah

Nā shobhate sabhāmadhye hansmadhye bakoh yathā

Those parents who do not educate their children are their enemies; for as is a crane among swans, so are ignorant children in a public assembly.

12. ॐ

Lālnād bahawo doshāstādnād bahawo gāunāh

Tasmātputram cha shishyam cha cha tādyenna tu lālyet

Love helps in developing many bad habits, while control and beating helps in learning discipline and in growing better. So one should chide or punish his son or pupil in place of showing love or over-indulgence.

13. ॐ

Slken wā tadarthen pādenaikāksharen wā

Abandhyam diwasam kuryād dānādhyayan karmabhih

One should not waste his time or life. One must read at least one or half or quarter of a *shloka* every day. Even learning a word a day will do. By studying, giving in charity or other pious deeds, one utilises one's life and time.

14. ॐ

Kāntāvyogah swajanapamānah rinasya sheshah kunripasya seva

Daridrabhao vishm sabhā cha bināgninaite pradahanti kāyam

If the given six kinds of evils inflict a person then they burn him even without fire:

- Separation from one's wife,
- Disgrace from one's own people,
- One's enemy saved in a battle,
- Forced to serve a wicked king,
- Poverty, and
- An ill-managed assembly that one arranges.

15. ॐ

Naditeere ta ye brikshah pargeheshu kāmini

Mantriheenāscha rājānah sheeghram nashyantyasansayam

The trees at the bank of rivers, a woman in another man's residence and a king without good counsel are readily destroyed.

16. ॐ

Balam vidyā cha viprānām rāgyā sainyam balam tathā

Balam bittam cha vaishyānām shudrānām paricharyakam

Learning is the strength of a Brahmin, a king's strength is in his army, a vaishya's strength is his wealth and a shudra's strength is in his spirit to serve.

17. ॐ

Nirdhanam purusham veshyā prajā bhagnam nripam tyajet

Khagā veetphalam briksham bhuktwā chā abhyāgatā griham

The prostitute forsakes a man without money, the subjects leave a king that cannot give security, the birds forsake a fruitless tree, and the unexpected guests leave a house after they have finished their meals.

18. ॐ

Grihitwa dakshinam viprāstyajanti yajmānakam

Prāptavidyāgurum shishyā dagdhā aranyam mrigāstathā

Brahmins leave their patrons after receiving sacred remuneration (*dakshinā*) from them, scholars leave their teachers after completing education from them, and animals (symbolised by a deer) leave a forest that has been burnt down.

19. ॐ

Durāchāri durdrishtirdurā āwasi cha durjanah

Yanmaitri kriyate pumibharnarah sheeghram vinasayati

He who befriends a man whose conduct is immoral, or with the one whose vision is impure or who is notoriously crooked, is ruined in no time.

20. ॐ

Sāmāne shobhate preetih rāgyi seva cha shobhate

Vānijyam vyāwahāreshu divyā stri shobhate grihe

Just like friendship flourishes between the equals, a service under a king is respectable and a gracious lady adds dignity to the home, it is good to be business-like in general relations.

Niti – 3

1. ॐ

Kasya doshah kule nāsti vyādhinā ko nā peeditah

Vyasanam kena nā prāptam kasya saukhyam nirantaram

In whose family tradition in this world, there is no blemish? Who is free from sickness and grief? Who is forever happy? There is some impurity in every family, each one is suffering from some disease and has some drawback. Naturally there is not a single person who is thoroughly happy.

2. ॐ

Āchārah kulamākhyāti deshamākhyati bhāshanam

Sambhramah snehamākhyāti vapurākhyāti bhojanam

The conduct of a person signifies his descent, one's country is known by one's language and pronunciation, one's love is expressed with the warmth he shows to others and his physique tells the quality and quantity of his food.

3. ॐ

Sukule yojayetkanyām putram vidyasu yojayet
Vyasane yjayetashatrum mitram dharma niyojayet

As a wise man, marry your daughter into a good family, give proper and adequate education to your son, make your enemy fall in bad habits and force your friend to follow religion.

4. ॐ

Durjanasya cha sarpasya varam sarpo nā durjanah
Sarpo dansahti kālen durjanastu pade pade

When there is question of selecting one between a serpent and a wicked person, select the serpent, for it stings at destined hour while the wicked bites at every step.

5. ॐ

Attadartha kulinānām nripāh kurvanti sangraham
Ādimadhyāvasāneshu nā tyajanti cha te nripam

The reason why the kings collect men of high qualities around them is that they do not leave him during his rise or fall.

6. ॐ

Pralaye bhinna maryādā bhawanti kil sāgarāh
Sāgarā bhedamichhanti pralaye api nā sādhawāh

At the time of the destruction of the Universe (*pralaya*), the seas break their limitations and delude all, while even at the time of great adversity, the sages and saintly men do not cross their limits.

7. ॐ

Murkhastu parihartabyah pratyaksho dwipadah pashuh

Bhinnati wakshalyena adrishtah kantako yathā

A fool is apparently an animal with two legs; he pierces the heart like an invisible thorn.

8. ॐ

Rupayoansampannah vishālkulsambhawah

Vidyāheenah nā sobhate nirgandhā ewa kinshukah

The uneducated men though endowed with beauty and youth and born in noble families are not liked like the flower devoid of sweet fragrance.

9. ॐ

Kokilānām swaro rupam strinām rupam pativratam

Vidyārupam kurupānām chhamā rupam tapaswinām

The beauty of a cuckoo is in its musical notes, that of a woman in her sincere devotion to her husband, that of an ugly person in his scholarship, and that of an ascetic in his forgiveness.

10. ॐ

Tyajedekam kulasyārthe grāmāsyārthe kulam tyajet

Grāmam janpadasyārthe ātmārthe prithivim tyajet

Forsake a member to save a family, leave a family to save a village, reject a village to save a country, and give up the whole earth for the sake of the self.

11. ॐ

Udyoge nāsti dāridryam japato nāsti pātakam

Moune cha kalaho nāsti nāsti jāgrite bhayam

Diligence overpowers poverty, chanting of the Name purifies a sinner, silence stops the fight and alertness frees from fear.

12. ॐ

Atirupena wai Sitā atigarbena Rāvanah

Atidānāt Balirbaddho ati sarbartra varjayet

Sita was kidnapped because of her unparalleled beauty, Ravana was killed because of his immense pride and Bali was ruined because of his extreme charitable nature. So, one must avoid extremity.

13. ॐ

Ko hi bhārah samarthānām kim duram vyavasāyinām

Ko videshah savidyānām kah parah priyavādinām

What is heavy for the strong and what place is distant for diligent people? What country is foreign to a learned man? Who is alien to a soft-spoken person?

14. ॐ

Ekenāpi subrkshena pushpitena sugandhinā

Wāsitam taddhanam suputrena kulam tathā

As the whole forest becomes fragrant by the blooming of a single tree, in the same way, a family earns fame and prestige by the birth cf one ideal son.

15. ॐ

Ekena shushkabrikshena dahyamānena dāhinā

Dyahate taddhanam sarvam kuputrena kulam tathā

As a single dry tree, if set aflame, causes the whole forest to burn, in the same way, one defiled son destroys the name, fame and wealth of a family.

16. ॐ

Ekenāpi suputrena vidyāyuktena sādhunā

Āhalāditam kulam sarvam yathā chandrena sharvari

A family feels delighted with one learned and virtuous son like the moon that brightens up the night.

17. ॐ

Kim jātairbahubhih putrai shokasantaptakārakaih

Baramekah kula awalambi yatra vishrāmyate kulam

What is the use of having many sons who give pain and grief? It is better to have only one son who fosters and leads the whole family.

18. ॐ

Lālyet panchvarshāni dashvarshāni tādyeta

Prāpte tu shodashe varshe putram mitrawatācharet

Show love and care to a son until he is five years of age, and control him for the next ten years, but treat him as a friend when he attains his sixteenth year.

19. ॐ

Upasarge anyachakre cha durbhikshe cha bhayāwahe

Asādhunjanasamparke yah palāyati sa jeewati

He who runs away from calamities, foreign invasions, terrible famines and the companionship of wicked men remains safe.

20. ॐ

Dharmārthakāmamokdhānām yasyaikoapi nā vidyate

One who has acquired none of the '*dharma*' (religious spirit), '*artha*' (economic independence), '*kāma*' (sensual satisfaction), and '*moksha*' (salvation or liberation), he only dies again and again in every life.

21. ॐ

Murkhā yatra nā pujyante dhānyam yatra susanchitam

Dampatayeh kalaho nāsti tatra shrih swayamāgatā

Where fools are not given respect and preference, where grain is stored well and where the husband and wife do not quarrel, there Lakshmi, the Goddess of wealth, comes of her own accord.

Niti – 4

1. ॐ

Āyuh karma cha vittam cha vidyā nidhanameva cha

Panchaitāni hi srijante garbhasthasyaiva dehinah

The lifespan, the type of work, wealth, learning and the time of death, all these five aspects are determined while one is in the womb.

2. ॐ

Sādhuvyaste nivartante puta mitrani bāndhwah

Ye cha taih sah gntārastaddharmātsukritam kulam

When a person becomes a saint, his children, friends and relatives flee away from him but those who live like him and follow him get respect and bring merit and fame to their families.

3. ॐ

Darshandhyānsansparshairmatsi kurmi cha pakshini
Shishu pālyate nityam tathā sajjansangatih

As fish, tortoise, and birds foster their young ones by sight, attention and touch, in the same way, the association of saintly men protects.

4. ॐ

Yāwatswastho hyam deho yāwanmrituscha duratah
Tāwad ātmahitam kuryat prānānte kim karisyati

As long as the body is healthy and active and death is far away, do the best for the self. What can one do when death overpowers?

5. ॐ

Kāmdhenugunā vidyā hyakāle phaldāyani
Prawase mātrisadrisini vidyā guptam dhanam smritam

Knowledge is the all fulfilling sacred cow which yields fruits in all seasons. It is like a mother when abroad. It is claimed to be the hidden treasure.

6. ॐ

Varmeko guni putro nirgunaischa shatairapi
Ekaschandrah tamo hanti nā cha tārā sahashtrashah

One ideal and virtuous son endowed with good qualities is far better than a hundred sons devoid of qualities, for the single moon dispels the darkness, while the numerous stars cannot.

7. ॐ

Murkhashchirāyujāto api tasmājjātamrito varah

Mritah sa chālpadukhāya yāwajjivam jado dahet

A stillborn son is far superior to a foolish son with a long life. The first causes grief for a moment while the latter keeps one in agony till he lives.

8. ॐ

Kugrāmvasah kulheenaseva kubhojanam krodhamukhi cha bhāryā

Putrashcha murkho vidhawa cha kanyā bināagninā shata pradahanti kāyam

All the following six continuously burn without fire — residing in a bad village devoid of facilities, serving a person of low family and character, eating unhealthy food, a fierce wife, a foolish son, and a widowed daughter.

9. ॐ

Kim tayā kriyate dhenwa yā nā dogdhri nā garvini

Koarthah putrena jātena yon a vidwān nā bhaktimān

As that cow is of no use that neither gives milk nor conceives, similarly, the birth of a son who neither learns nor turns to be devotee is meaningless.

10. ॐ

Samsāra tāpadagdhānām trayo vishrānti hetawah

Apatyam cha kalatram cha satām sangatireva cha

There are three things in the world which give relief to an agonised soul. They are offspring, a wife, and the company of devotees.

11. ॐ

Sakrijjalpanti rājānah sakrijjalpanti panditāh

Sakrit kanyā pradiyante triyetāni sakritsakrit

Kings and men of learning speak once, and the daughter is given in marriage once. These three things happen once and only once.

12. ॐ

Ekākinā tapo dwābhyām pathanam gāyanam tribhih

Chaturbhirgamanam chhetram panchabhirbahubhiranah

Austerities should be practised alone, two should study together, three can sing in a chorus, four persons can undertake a journey, five can be engaged in agriculture and many should fight a battle together.

13. ॐ

Sā bhāryā yā shuchirdakshā sā bhāryā yā pativratā

Sā bhāryā yā patipritā sā bhāryā satyavādini

A true wife is she who is clean and an expert in her work, who is chaste, pleasing to her husband and truthful.

14. ॐ

Aputrasya griham shunyam dishah shunyāstwabāndhawāh
Murkhasya hridayam shunyam sarvashunyā daridratā

A house without a child is a void, the directions are void without relatives, the heart of a fool is a void and in poverty everything is a void.

15. ॐ

Unabhyāse visham shastram jeerne bhojanam visham
Daridrasya visham goshthi vridhasya taruni visham

Scriptures are poison, if not put into practice, a sumptuous meal is poison to a patient, a social gathering is poison to a poor person, and a young wife is poison to an aged man.

16. ॐ

Tyajedadharmam dayāheenam vidyāheenam gurum tyajet
Tyajetkrodhamukhi bhāryām nihsnehān bāndhawānstyalet

Abandon the religion which is without compassion and mercy. Leave a guru without knowledge. Reject the wife with an angry attitude and forsake the relatives who are without affection.

17. ॐ

Adhwā jarā manusyānām vājinām bandhanam jarā
Amaithunam jarā strinām vastrānām ātapo jarā

Constantly travelling on foot brings old age early upon a man, a horse becomes old easily by being left tied up constantly, a woman gets old early if denied sensual contact, and clothes wear out quickly if left in the sun regularly.

18. ॐ

Kah kālah kāni mitrāni ko deshah kau vyaya āgamau

Kashchāham kā me shaktiriti chityam muhurmuhuh

A wise man should usually keep on thinking about his time, his friends, the place, his income, expenditure, what is he and from where he derives power?

19. ॐ

Janitā chopanetā cha yastu vidyām pryachchhati

Annadātā bhayatrātā panchaite pitarah smritā

The following five have been accepted as fathers — he who is responsible for birth, he who baptises with the sacred thread, the teacher who imparts education, one who gives food and one who keeps free from fear.

20. ॐ

Rājpatni guroh patni mitrapatni tathaiva cha

Patnimātā swamātā cha panchaitā mātarah smritāh

The following five have been accepted as mothers — the wife of the king, the wife of the guru, the mother of a friend, the mother of one's wife and one's own mother.

21. ॐ

Agnirdevo dwijātinām muninām hridi daivatam
Pratimā swalpbuddhinām sarbatra samdarshinah

Brahmin, *kshatriya* and *vaishya* are called *dwij*. Their God is Fire (*yajna*). The Supreme Lord of saints, *munis* and devotees resides in their heart, for the ignorant and fools the idol is the God and those who have a balanced view see God at every place.

Niti – 5

1. ॐ

Gururagnidwijātinām varnānām brahmano guruh

Patireva guruh strinām sarbasyā abhyāgato guruh

Agni, the Fire God, is respectable and should be worshipped as guru by Brahmin, *kshatriya* and *vaishya* who get the second birth. Brahmins are the guru and should be worshipped by other castes. The husband is the guru and should be worshipped by his wife, and the guest who comes to a family is the guru and should be worshipped by all the members.

2. ॐ

Yathā chaturbhih kanakam parikshayate nigharshana cha chhedantāptādanaih

Tathā chaturbhih purush parikshayate tyāgena sheelena gunena karmanā

As gold is tested in four ways by rubbing, cutting, heating and beating, in the same way a man is tested by his renunciation, conduct, qualities and actions.

3. ॐ

Tāwad bhayeshu bhetavyam yāwadbhayamnāgtam
Āgatam tu bhayam dristwā prahartabyam shankayā

Dangers lurk upon everyone and people are usually afraid of them. Such things should be dreaded till they have not overtaken someone, but once they have come, one must try to overpower them without hesitation and with all might.

4. ॐ

Ekodarsamudbhutā ek nakshatra jātakāh
Nā bhawanti samāh sheele yathā badarikantakāh

Though born from the same womb and under the same stars, persons are different in nature and disposition as the thousands of fruits and thorns of a *bair* (berry) tree are not the same.

5. ॐ

Nihspriho nā adhikāri syānnākāmi mandanpriyah
Nā abidagdhah priyam bruyāt sphutavaktā nā vanchakah

The hands of the office bearers are never clean, he who is clean does not like to hold an office. The sensual persons use cosmetics, he who has no physical desires does not care for bodily decorations. He who is not wise cannot be soft-spoken, and he who speaks out plainly and boldly cannot be a deceiver.

6. ॐ

Murkhānām panditā dweshyā adhanānām mahādhanā
Barāhanganāh kulstrinām subhagānām cha durbhagāh

The foolish envy the learned, the poor envy the rich, a prostitute envies a righteously married lady and the ugly ones envy the beautiful ladies.

7. ॐ

Alpsyopahatā vidyā parhastagatāh dtriyah
Alpbeejam hatam kshetram sainyamanāyakam

Indolent application ruins knowledge in the same way as a woman is lost under the control of others, a land is ruined with sparsely sown seeds, and an army is lost for the want of a commander.

8. ॐ

Abhyāsāddhāryate vidyā kulam sheelena dhāryate
Gunena gyāyate twāryah kopo netrena gamyate

Knowledge is retained through constant practice, the prestige of the family is maintained through moral conduct, a respectable person is recognised by his excellent qualities, and anger is visible in the eyes.

9. ॐ

Vittena rakshyate dharmo vidyā yogena rakshyate
Mridunā rakshyate bhupah satstriyām rakshyate graham

Religion is preserved by wealth, knowledge by diligent practice, a king can be saved by sweet conciliatory words, and a home is saved by a dutiful housewife.

10. ॐ

Anyathā vedapāndityam shāstramāchāramanyathā
Anyathā kuvachah shāntam lokāh klishyanti cha anyathā

Those who blaspheme Vedic wisdom, ridicule the life led according to the *shāstras*, and who deride men of peaceful temperament, come to grief. They never get benefit out of it.

11. ॐ

Dāridryanāshanam dānam sheelam durgati nāshanam
Agyaānnāshni pragyā bhāvanā bhaināshini

Charity puts an end to poverty, righteous conduct gets one out of misery, wisdom destroys ignorance and confidence overcomes fear.

12. ॐ

Nāsti kāmasamo vyādhih nāsti mohasamo ripuh
Nāsti kopasamo vanhih nāsti gyānāt param sukham

There is no disease as destructive as lust, no enemy as dangerous as infatuation, no fire as devastating as wrath, and no happiness as blissful as spiritual knowledge.

13. ॐ

Janmamrityu hi yātyeko bhunaktyekah shubha ashubham
Narkeshu patatyeka eko yāti parām gatim

A man is born alone and alone he dies, one experiences the consequences of one's good and bad deeds alone, one goes to the hell or gets salvation for the self alone.

14. ॐ

Trnam brahmavidah swargastrinam shurasya jeevitam

Jitāshashya trinam nāri nispriham trinam jagat

Heaven is but a straw to him who leads a spiritual life and knows the Brahma, life is like a straw to a valiant man, a woman is but a straw to him who has subdued his senses, and the Universe is like a straw to him who is detached from the world.

15. ॐ

Vidyā mitram pravāsheshu bhāryā mitram griheshu cha

Vyādhitasyaushadham mitram dharmo mitram mritasya cha

Learning is a friend outside one's home, the wife is a friend at home, medicine is a friend in sickness, and religious merit is the only friend to a dead person.

16. ॐ

Brithābrishtih samudreshu brithātripteshu bhojanam

Brithādānam dhanādhyeshu brithā deepo diwāpi cha

Rain in the oceans is useless, food to the satiated is useless, charity to the one who is wealthy is meaningless, and a burning lamp during the daytime is total wastage.

17. ॐ

Nāstimeghasamam toyam nāsti cha ātmasamam balam

Nāsti chakshuh samam tejo nāsti dhānyasamam priyam

Rainwater is the purest water, one's own strength is the best strength, nothing is brighter than the light of the eyes, and no wealth is dearer than food grain.

18. ॐ

Adhanā dhanamichhanti vācham chaiva chatuspadāh
Mānawāh swargamichhanti mokashamichhanti devatāh

The poor wish for wealth, animals wish for the power to speak, men wish for heaven, and godly persons wish for liberation.

19. ॐ

Satyena dhāryate prithvi satyena tapate rabih
Satyena wāti vāyushcha sarvam satye pratisthitam

The earth has the support of truth, the hot sun shines by truth, the truth makes the winds blow; in fact, all things rest upon truth.

20. ॐ

Chalā laxmischalāh prānāschalam jeevit yauvanam
Chalāchale cha samsāre dharm eko hi nishchalah

The Goddess of wealth (Lakshmi) is active (*chanchala*), and so is our breath. The duration of life and youth is uncertain, and the place of habitation too is unstable; in this moving and unstable world, religion alone is immovable.

21. ॐ

Narānām nāpito dhurtah pakshinām chaiva vayasah
Chatuspadām srigālastu strinām dhurtah cha mālini

Among men, the barber is the most cunning. Among birds, the crow is the wisest. Among beasts, the jackal is really intelligent, and among women the flower girl (*mālin*) is the wittiest.

Niti – 6

1. ॐ

Shrutwā dharmam vijānāti shrutwā tyaja durmatim
Shrutwā gyānam āpnoti shrutwā mokashamawāpnuyāt

By listening to the scriptures one understands *dharma*, after hearing the moral lessons one forsakes malignity and egocentricity, by listening to the books of knowledge one acquires wisdom, and by listening to and following the dictates one gets liberation from worldly bondage of life and death.

2. ॐ

Pakshinānām kākaschāndālah pashunām chaiva kukurah
Muninām kopi chāndālah sarbesām chaiva nindakah

Among birds the crow is the vilest, among beasts the dog, the ascetic who shows anger, and among the mass, the one he who blasphemes others is the vilest creature (*chāndāla*).

3. ॐ

Bhasmanā shudhyate kānsyam tāmramamamalen shudhayati
Rajasa shudhayate nāri nadi begena shudhayati

Brass is purified and polished by ashes, copper is cleaned and brightened by tamarind, a woman cleaned by her menses is turned healthier, and a river is cleaned and purified by its flow.

4. ॐ

Bhraman sampujyate rājā bhraman sampujayate dwijah
Bhraman sampujyate yogi stri bhramanti vinashayati

The king, the Brahmins, and the ascetics and *yogis* are respected when they move from place to place, but the woman who wanders is completely ruined.

5. ॐ

Yasyārthātasya mitrāni yasyārthātasya bāndhwāh
Yasyārthāh sa pumānlloke yasyārthāh sa cha panditah

He who has wealth has friends. He who is wealthy has relatives. The rich one alone is called a man, and the affluent alone is respected as a pandit.

6. ॐ

Tādrishi jāyate buddhirvyavasāyoapi tadrishah
Sahāyastādrishā yewa yādrishi bhabitavyatā

As is the Providence and fate of a person, his intellect functions accordingly and he selects his activities according to his future and fate, and by the will of Providence, one does the things and is surrounded by helpers.

7. ॐ

Kālah pachati bhutāni kālah sangharate prajāh

Kālah supteshu jāgarti kālo hi durratikramah

Time perfects all living beings as well as kills them; it alone is awake when all others are asleep. Time is insurmountable.

8. ॐ

Nā pashyati cha janmāndhah kāmāndho nā pashyati

Nā pashyati madonamatto hyarthi doshān nā pashyati

Those born blind cannot see, those in the grip of sensual urge also cannot see, proud men and egoists cannot distinguish between good and evil, and those bent upon acquiring riches see no sin in their actions.

9. ॐ

Swayam karma karotyātmā swayam tatphalamashanute

Swayam bhramati samsāre swayam tasmādwimuchayate

Man himself does the *karma* and he himself suffers from its good and bad results thereby. By his own actions he entangles himself in the world (*samsāra*), and by his own efforts he extricates himself and gets liberation from the wheel of birth and death.

10. ॐ

Rājā rāshtrakritam bhukte rāgyah pāpam purohitah

Bhartā cha strikritam pāpam shishya pāpam gurustathā

The king has to suffer for the sins of his subjects, the priest (*purohita*) suffers for the misdeeds of the king, a husband suffers for the acts of his wife, and the guru suffers for the foolishness of his pupils.

11. ॐ

Rinkartā pitā shatru mātā cha vyabhichārani

Bhāryā rupawati shatruh putrah shatruh apanditah

A father who is under loans is an enemy, an adulterous mother is an enemy, a beautiful wife is an enemy, and a foolish son is also an enemy.

12. ॐ

Lubdhamarthena grihaniyāt stabdhamanjali karmanā

Murkha chhando anubritena yathārthatwena panditam

One should try to please and turn a lustful man to his side by offering him a gift, an obstinate man with folded hands, a fool by obeying him, and a learned man by revealing the truth.

13. ॐ

Baram nā rājyam nā kurājarājyam baram nā mitram nā kumitramitram

Baram nā shishyo nā kushishyashishyo baram nā dārā nā kudārdārāh

It is better to be without a kingdom than to rule over a weak and petty kingdom. It is better to be without a friend than to have a rascal as a friend. It is better to be without a disciple than to have a bad and stupid pupil, and it is better to be without a wife than to have an adulterous one.

14. ॐ

Kurājarājyena kutah prajāsukham kumitramitrena kuto asti nibritih

Kudārdārāscha kuto grihe ratih kushishyamadhyāpayatah kuto yashah

The people cannot be happy under an ill-managed kingdom. One cannot get peace from a rascal friend. One cannot live happily with an adulterous wife, one cannot get fame and respect by teaching an unworthy disciple.

15. ॐ

Snhādekam bakādekam shikshechtwāri kukkutāt

Vāyasātpancha shikshecha shat shunastrini gardabhāt

Learn one thing from a lion and one from a crane, four from a cock, five from a crow, six from a dog and three from an ass.

(Chanakya has discussed what we can learn from the animals mentioned in *shloka* 15 in the next four *shlokas*.)

16. ॐ

Prabhutam kāryamalpam wā yannarah kartumichhati

Sarbhārambhena tatkaryam sinhādekam prachakshate

One excellent thing we can learn from a lion is to make a whole-hearted and strenuous effort at the start of whatever one wishes to accomplish.

17. ॐ

Indriyāni cha sanyamya bakwat pandito narah

Deshakālabalam gyātwā sarbakāryāni sādhayet

The wise man should restrain his senses and accomplish his purpose with utmost concentration on the objective just like a crane.

18. ॐ

Pratyuthānam cha yuddham cha samvibhāgam cha bandhushu

Swayamākramya bhuktam ch shikshechatwāri kukkutāt

To wake at the proper time, to be always ready to fight, to make a fair division of the available food among relations, and to earn one's bread by personal effort are the four things that we can learn from a cock.

19. ॐ

Gurhamaithunacharitwam cha kāle kāle cha sangraham
Apramattamaviswāsam panch shikshecha vāyasāt

Cardinal union in secrecy, to be bold, to store something from time to time, to be alert all the time, and not to trust anyone fully — these five things should be learnt from a crow.

20. ॐ

Bahwāshi swalpsantushtah sunidro laghuchetanah
Swāmibhaktacha shurashcha shadete shwānto gunāh

To be content with the least available food despite intense hunger, to awaken instantly although in deep slumber, faithfulness towards the master, and great fighting spirit — these qualities should be learnt from dogs.

21. ॐ

Sushrāntoapi wahed bhāram sheetoshnam nā cha pashyati
Santushtascharate nityam trini shikshecha gardabhāt

Although tired yet continue to carry the burden, to be unmindful of cold and heat, and to be always contented — these three things should be learnt from an ass.

22. ॐ

Ha aitān vinshatigunānācharishyati mānawah
Kāryāvasthāsu sarvāsu ajeyah sa bhabishyati

He who would learn and bring these twenty virtues into constant practice shall become invincible in all his undertakings and in every situation.

Niti – 7

1. ॐ

Arthanāsham manastāspam grihe dushcharitāni cha

Vanchanam cha apamānam cha matimān nā prakāshyet

A wise man should not reveal the loss of wealth, the mental agony, the misconduct at home, abusive language used by others, and disgrace that he had to face.

2. ॐ

Dhandhānprayogeshu vidyāsangrahaneshu cha

Āhāre vyavahāre cha tyaktalajjah sukhi bhawet

He who gives up shyness in financial dealings, in acquiring knowledge, in eating and in social dealings, becomes happy.

3. ॐ

Santoshāmrita triptānām yatsukham shāntachetasām
Nā cha tad dhanlubdhānāmitashchetashcha dhāwatām

He who is satiated with the nectar of contentment gets that rare bliss which is never attained by greedy persons who move here and there for wealth.

4. ॐ

Santoshastrishu kartavyah swadāre bhojane dhane
Trisu chaiva nā kartavyo adhyayane tapadānayoh

One should feel satisfied with his wife, food that he gets and wealth acquired by honest means and effort. On the other hand, one should never feel satisfied with the study, chanting of the holy Name and charity.

5. ॐ

Viprayorviprahyoshcha dampatyoh swāmibhrityoh
Antarena nā gantavyam halasya brishabhasya cha

One should not pass between two Brahmins, between a Brahmin and his sacrificial fire, between a wife and her husband, a master and his servant, and a plough and the oxen.

6. ॐ

Pādābhyām nā sprishedagnim gurum brahmineva cha
Naiva gām nā kumārim cha nā bridham nā shishum tathā

Avoid touching fire, the spiritual master or a Brahmin with foot, but never touch with your feet a cow, a virgin, an old man and a child.

7. ॐ

Shakatam panchahastena dashahastena vājinam
Hast shatahasten deshatyāgena durjanam

One should think of one's safety first and hence one should maintain a distance of five cubits from a bullock cart, ten cubits from a horse and hundred cubits from an elephant but to get rid of a wicked person one should even leave that place or country.

8. ॐ

Hasti ankushmātrena waji hastena tādyate
Shringi lagudahastena khangahastena durjanah

An elephant is controlled by a goad (*ankusha*), a horse by a slap of the hand, a horned animal with a stick, and a bad element with a sword.

9. ॐ

Tushyanti bhojane biprā mayurā ghanagarjite
Sādhavah parsampatau khalahparvipattishu

Brahmins find pleasure and satisfaction in a good meal, peacocks in the rains and thunder of clouds, a saint in the wealth and prosperity of others, and the wicked in the suffering and misery of others.

10. ॐ

Anulomena balinam pratilomena balina durjanam
Ātmatulya balam shatrum vinayena balena wa

Be friendly and win or conciliate a stronger enemy by friendly relations or submission, but meet a wicked enemy with greater force or opposition, and win by politeness or force as required while dealing with such enemies who are equal to you in power.

11. ॐ

Bāhubeerya balam rāgyo brāhmno brahmvid bali
Rupayauvanamādhuryam strinām balamuttamam

The power of a king lies in his mighty arms and fighting ability, that of a Brahmin in his spiritual and cosmic knowledge, and that of a woman in her beauty, youthfulness and sweetness.

12. ॐ

Nā atyantam saralairbhābyam gatwā pashya vanasthaleem
Chhidyante saralāstatra kubjāstishthanti pādapāh

It is not beneficial to be simple or to be upright. It is self-destructive. Go to the forest and see for yourself that straight trees are cut down early and easily, while the crooked and hunchbacked stand untouched.

13. ॐ

Yatrodakam tatra basanti hansah tathaiva shushkam parivarjayanti
Nā hansatulyena narena bhābyam punastyajante punarāshrayante

Wherever there is water, swans live there and they immediately leave the place as soon as the water dries up; a man should not be selfish like them and should not act so, for he may be forced to return to such men or places that he had left.

14. ॐ

Upārjitām vittānām tyāga awa hi rakshanam

Tadāgodarasansthānām pariwāh evā ambhasām

Accumulated wealth is saved by spending reasonably well on living or in business or in charity or by investing it profitably. Saving accumulated wealth is just as a reservoir kept fresh by letting out the stagnant water.

15. ॐ

Yasyārthāstasya mitrāni yasyārthāstasya bandhavāh

Yasyārthāh sa pumānloke yasyārthāh sa cha jeevati

He who has wealth has friends and relatives; he alone survives and is given due respect.

16. ॐ

Swargasthitānāmih jeevaloke chatwāri chinhāni basanti dehe

Dānprasango madhurā cha vāni devārchanam brahamantarpanam

Those born after residing in heaven possess the following four qualities — they believe in charity, speak sweetly, show devotion and satisfy the needs of Brahmins.

17. ॐ

Atyantakopah katukā cha vāni daridratā cha swajaneshu vairam

Neechprasangah kulaheenaseva chinhāni dehe narakasthitānām

Those born after residing in heaven possess the following four qualities — they are extremely wrathful, use harsh words, show enmity to their relatives, serve the men of low birth and keep the company of the base.

18. ॐ

Gamyate yadi mrigenra mandiram labhyate karikapolamauktikam

Jambukā alayagate cha prāpyte vatsapuchhakharacharmakhandanam

If one dares, one can extract the pearls from the head of elephants, enter the den of a lion, but by going inside the hole of a jackal what one can get except the tail of a calf or the hide of an ass.

19. ॐ

Shunah puchhameva vyartham jeevitam vidyā binā

Nā guhyagopane shaktam nā cha dunshaniwārane

The life of an uneducated man is as useless as that tail of a dog, which neither can cover its organs, nor can protect it from the bites of flies and mosquitoes.

20. ॐ

Vāchah shaucham cha manasah shauchamindriyanigrahah

Sarvabhute dayā shaucham atadchhautram parārthinām

Purity of speech, a mind that controls the senses, compassion for all living beings, and wealth earned through piety are the characteristics of those who are to get salvation.

21. ॐ

Pushpe gandham tile tailam kāstheagnim payasi ghritam

Ikachhau gudam tathā dehe pashyā ātmānam vivekatah

As there is fragrance in flowers, oil in the sesame seeds, fire in wood, pure *ghee* in milk, and sweetness in sugarcane, so the God and the spirit reside in our body. The wise should make an endeavour to know the soul and the God.

Niti – 8

1. ॐ

Adhamā dhanamichchhanti dhanam mānama cha madhyamā
Uttamā mānamichchhanti māno hi mahatām dhanam

Unmodified lower level people wish to get only wealth, a bit refined men at the middle level wish for both wealth and honour, while the most refined people of the highest level wish only for the honour, for honour is the greatest and the most precious wealth.

2. ॐ

Ekshurāpah payo mulam tambulam phalamaushadham
Bhakshayitwāpi kartavyāh snānadānā ādikāh kriyāh

It is usually believed that religious deeds can be performed before eating a thing and only after taking the bath but this *shloka* claims that after taking sugarcane, water, milk, roots, beetle, fruits and medicines, one can take a bath and engage in charity works.

3. ॐ

Deepo bhakshyante āntam kajjalam cha prasuyate

Yadannam bhakshayannityam jāyate tādrishi prajā

The lamp eats up the darkness and therefore it produces blackened soot and smoke; in the same way, the nature and quality of our food determines the nature and qualities of our children.

4. ॐ

Vittam dehi gunānwiteshu matimannānyatra dehi kwachit

Prāptam wārinidherjalam ghanmukhe mādhuryayuktam sadā

Jeevānsthāwerjangāmānshcha sakalān sanjeevya bhumandalam

Bhuyah pashya tadeva kotigunitam gachchhantamambhonidham

O wise man! Give wealth only to the wise, worthy and to men with qualities, but never to the fools, unworthy and to men devoid of qualities. The salty water of the sea purified by the sun and stored in the clouds always becomes sweet. The rainwater gives life to and enlivens all living beings (both movable and immovable) on the earth, and again returns back to the ocean. It means that the wealth given to someone with qualities is returned in various ways.

5. ॐ

Chāndālānām sahastre cha suribhistatwadarshibhih

Eko hi yawanah prokto nā neecho yawanāt parah

The wise who know and understand the essence of the scriptures and life have declared that one *yavana*, is equal in slyness to a thousand *chāndālas*, and hence a *yavana* is the worst creature; indeed, there is none more dastardly than him.

6. ॐ

Tailā abhyange chitādhume maithune kshourkarmani

Tāwad bhawati chāndālo yāwatsnānam nā cha ācharet

One must take a bath after rubbing oil on the body, after getting mixed with smoke from a funeral pyre, after sex and after being shaved, for one remains a *chāndāla* till one takes a bath after any such situations.

7. ॐ

Ajeerne bhesajam wāri jeerne wāri balapradam

Bhojane cha amritam wāri bhojanānte bishpradam

Water is medicine during indigestion; it is invigorating. When the food taken is well digested, then water gives energy. Water is like nectar when drunk after half of the food is consumed, but it is poison when taken at the end of a meal.

8. ॐ

Hatam gyānam kriyāheenam hataschā agyānto narah
Hatam nirnāyakam sainyam striyo nashtā hyabhartrikāh

Knowledge is lost without being put into practice, a man is lost because of ignorance, an army is lost without a commander, and a woman is lost without a husband.

9. ॐ

Vriddhakā mritā bhāryā bandhuhaste gatah dhanam
Bhojanam cha parādhinam tisrah punsām vidambanāh

He is really very unfortunate who faces the death of his wife during old age, is forced to give his money to his relatives or depends on others for food.

10. ॐ

Nāgnihotram binā vidyā nā cha dānam binā kriyā
Nā bhāwena binā siddhistasmādbhāwo hi kāranam

Chanting of the Vedas is rendered useless without making ritualistic sacrifices through *Agni* (*Agnihotra*), and sacrifices are futile if not followed by charity and gifts (*dān-dakshinā*). There is no success without faith and devotion.

11. ॐ

Kāshthapāshānadhātunām kritwā bhāwena sevanam
Shradhya cha tayā siddhastasya Vishnuh prasidati

If the statue of wood, stone or metal is accepted as the Lord and worshipped with faith and devotion, success is bound to come for Lord Vishnu is pleased with his devotees.

12. ॐ

Nā devo vidyate kāshthe nā pāshāne nā mrinmaye

Bhāwe hi vidyate devastasmād bhāwo hi kāranam

God is not there in a statue of wood or stone or some dead material. He is in acceptance and feelings. He appears and exists wherever He is accepted to exist and worshipped.

13. ॐ

Shāntitulyam tapo nāsti nā santoshātparam sukham

Nā trishnayā paro vyādhih nā cha dharmo dayā parah

There is no austerity equal to a peaceful and serene mind, and there is no happiness equal to contentment. In the same way there is no disease like lust and covetousness, and there is no greater religion and virtue like sympathy, compassion, kindness or mercy.

14. ॐ

Krodho vaivawasto rājā trishnā vaitarani nadi

Vidyā kāmdudhā dhenuh santosho nandanam vanam

Anger is like *Yamarāja* (the god of death), thirst is like the river *Vaitarani* (the river of hell), knowledge is like a *Kāmadhenu* (the all-giving cow), and contentment is like *Nandanavana* (the garden of *Indraloka*).

15. ॐ

Guno bhushayate rupam sheelam bhushayate kulam
Siddhirbhushayate vidyām bhogo bhushayate dhanam

Excellent qualities are ornaments for personal appearance, righteous and moral conducts are the ornaments for family traditions, success and performances are ornaments to learning, and proper and wise utilisation is the ornament of wealth.

16. ॐ

Nirgunasya hatam rupam duhsheelasya hatam kulam
Asiddhasya hatā vidyā abhogena hatam dhanam

Lack of qualities spoils beauty, immoral conduct destroys the noble family tradition, knowledge goes in vain if not used properly and successfully, and wealth is ruined if not utilised.

17. ॐ

Shuchirbhumigatam toyam shuddhā nāri patibratā
Shuchih kshemkaro rājā santoshi Brahminh shuchi

Water seeped into the earth is pure, and pure is a dedicated wife, the king who works for the welfare of his people is pure, and pious and happy is the Brahmin who is contented.

18. ॐ

Asantushtā dwijā nashtāh santushtāscha mahibhritah
Salajja ganikā nastā nirlajjascha kulanganā

Discontented Brahmins and contented kings are destroyed, shy prostitutes and shameless housewives are ruined.

19. ॐ

Kim kulena vishālena vidyāhinena dehinām
Duskulinoapi vidwānscha devairapi supujyate

Of what avail is a high birth if a person is devoid of scholarship? A scholar of low birth is also honoured even by the gods.

20. ॐ

Vidwān prashasyate loke vidwān gachchhati gauravam
Vidyā labhate sarvam vidyā sarvatra pujyate

A learned man is honoured by the people. A learned man commands respect everywhere for his learning. Indeed, knowledge gives everything as learning is honoured everywhere.

21. ॐ

Mānsbhakshaih surāpānairmurkhaischāksharavarjitaih
Pashubhih purushākārairbhārā ākrantā cha medani

The earth remains aggrieved and in agony with the weight of non-vegetarians, drunkards, fools and illiterate men-like animals.

22. ॐ

Annahino daheda rāshtram mantrahinashcha ritwijah
Yajamānam dānhino nāsti yagyasamo ripuh

There is no enemy like a *yajna* which makes the kingdom grainless, which has such *mantra* chanters who know no *mantras*, and which is organised by such a man (*yajamān*) who is devoid of the sense of charity.

Niti – 9

1. ॐ

Muktimichhasi chetāta vishayān vishavat tyaj

Kshamā ārjawam dayā shoucham satyam peeyushavad bhaj

If you wish to get salvation, then be free from the addictions, get away from physical pleasure, think them to be poison and abandon them. Accept forbearance, upright conduct, mercy, cleanliness and truth as nectar and make them a part of your life.

2. ॐ

Parasperasya marmāni ye bhāshante narādhamāh

Ta yewam vilayam yānti valmikodar sarpwat

Those who open the secrets of others destroy themselves as a serpent that is destroyed by the ants in an anthill.

3. ॐ

Gandhah suvarhe phalamikshudande
Nā ākāri pushpam khalu chandanasya
Vidwān dhanādhyascha nripaschirāyuh
Dhātuh purā koapi nā buddhoabhut

Gold has no perfume, sugarcane has no fruit, sandalwood has no flowers, the learned are not wealthy and the king does not have a long life. Perhaps there was none to advise Brahma, the creator.

4. ॐ

Sarva aushadhināmamritā pradhānā sarbeshu soukhyeswashanam pradhānam
Sarbe indriyānām nayanam pradhānam sarbeshu gātreshu shirah pradhānam

Nectar (*amrita*) is the best among medicines, food is the best among the types of physical pleasure, the eye is the best among the organs, and the head is the best among the parts of body.

5. ॐ

Duto nā sancharati khe nā chachcha vārtā
Purvam nā jalpitamidam nā cha sangamo asti
Vyomni sthitam ravi-shashi grahanam prashashtam
Jānāti wo dwijbarah sa katham nā vidwāna

Messengers do not move in the sky and conversation is not possible in the space. A contact cannot be established with them. Why can that Brahmin not be accepted as learned who predicts the eclipse of the sun and moon?

6. ॐ

Vidyārthi sevakah pānthah kshudhārator bhayakātarah
Bhāndāri ratihāri cha sapt suptāna prabodhayet

Students, servants, travellers, hungry persons, frightened people, stewards and watchmen ought to be wakened if they fall asleep.

7. ॐ

Ahim nripam cha shārdulam kitim cha bālakam tathā
Parswānam cha murkham cha sapta suptān nā bodhayet

The serpent, the king, the tiger, the wasp, the kids, the dog of other people, and the fool ought not to be wakened from sleep.

8. ॐ

Arthā adhitāshcha yairvedāstathā shudrānnabhojināh
Te dwijah kim karishyanti nirvishā eva pannagāh

Such Brahmins who studied Vedas for material gain, and such men who eat the food earned by *Shudras*, lack potency and are unable to do anything important, for they are like serpents without fangs.

9. ॐ

Yasmina ruste bhayam nāsti tushte naiva dhanā āgamah
Nigraho anugraho nāsti sa rustam kim karishyati

They, whose anger rouses no fear and whose pleasure confers no favour in the form of material reward, are powerless entity. When pleased if he cannot protect, then what can he do if and when angry?

10. ॐ

Nirvishenāpi sarpena kartavyā mahati phanā

Vishamastu nā cha apyastu ghatātopo bhayankarah

Even without poison a serpent must raise its hood wide and high. The people know nothing about its poison. The exhibition of terror will be enough to keep them away.

11. ॐ

Prātadyurtaprasangena madhyānhe strprasangatah

Rātrou chourprasangena kalogachchhatyadhimtām

The fools waste their morning in gambling, noon with women and their night in stealing.

12. ॐ

Swahastagrathitāmālā swahastadhristachandanam

Swahastalikhitastotram shakrashyāpi shriyam haret

By preparing a garland for a Deity with one's own hands, by grinding sandalwood paste for the Lord with one's own hands; and by writing sacred prayers with one's own mind, one gets the blessing and wealth of Indra.

13. ॐ

Ikshudandāstilā kshudrāh kāntā hema cha medani

Chandanam dahi tāmbulam mardanam gunavardhanam

The more the sugarcane, sesame seeds, fools, low-quality people, women, gold, sandalwood, curd and betel are molested, the better becomes their taste or quality.

14. ॐ

Daridratā dheertayā virājate kuvastratā shubhratayā virājate

Kadannatā choshantayā virājate kurupatā sheeltayā virājate

Poverty will not be painful if it is faced with patience, ordinary garments will not look shabby if kept and worn clean, junk food will not be harmful if eaten freshly cooked and warm, and ugliness will not be painful if balanced by sweet, moral and pleasing behaviour.

Niti – 10

1. ॐ

Dhanheeno nā heenashcha dhanikah sa sunishchayah

Vidyāratnena yo heenah sa heenah sarvavastushu

Lack of wealth does not make a man poor. One is rich if he is learned but the man devoid of learning is destitute in every way.

2. ॐ

Dristiputam nyaset pādam bastraputam pibejjalam

Shāstraputam vaded vākyam manah putam samacharet

One should look well before taking another step, one should filter water with a cloth before drinking it, one should ascertain first then speak according to the scriptures and one should act after thinking carefully.

3. ॐ

Sukhārthi wā tyajedvidyām vidyārthi wā tyajet sukham
Sukhārthinah kuto vidyā vidyārthinah kuto sukham

If one wishes to enjoy physical pleasure he should give up the idea of acquiring knowledge, if one wishes to get knowledge he should not think of physical pleasure. Those who seek pleasure cannot acquire knowledge those who seek knowledge cannot get pleasure.

4. ॐ

Kavayah kim nā pashyanti kim nā kurbanti yoshitah
Madyapāh kim nā jalpanti kim nā bhakshanti vāyasāh

What is it that the poets cannot see through their power of imagination? What is that the women are incapable of doing? What is it that drunken people cannot say? What is there that a crow would not eat?

5. ॐ

Rankam karoti rājānam rājānam rankmewa cha
Dhaninam nirdhanam chaiwa nirdhanam dhaninam vidhih

Fate makes a beggar out of a king and changes a beggar into a king. It makes a rich man poor and a poor man rich.

6. ॐ

Lubadhānām yāchakah shatruh murkhānām bodhakah ripuh
Jārshtrinām patih shatruh chorānām chandrā ripuh

A beggar is an enemy to a miser, a wise counsellor is the enemy to fools, an adulterous wife's enemy is her husband, and the moon is the enemy of the thief.

7. ॐ

Yeshām nā vidyā nā tapo nā dānam nā gyānam nā sheelam nā guno nā dharmah

Te martyaloke bhuwi bhārbhutā manusyarupena mrigāscharanti

Those who have neither education nor penance, neither the sense to give nor knowledge, neither good moral character, virtue, benevolence nor religious nature are a burden on the earth; they are like wild animals wandering in the form of men.

8. ॐ

Antahsārvihinānāmupadesho nā jāyete

Malayāchal sansargāt nā venushchandanāyate

Those that are empty-minded cannot be benefited by teachings. Bamboo does not acquire the quality of sandalwood by growing on the Malaya Mountain.

9. ॐ

Yasya nāsti swayam pragyā shāstram tasya karoti kim

Lochanābhyām vihinasya darpanah kim karishyati

What good can the scriptures do to a man who has no knowledge of his own? Of what use is a mirror to a blind man?

10. ॐ

Durjanam sajjanam kartumupāyo nā hi bhutale

Apānam shatadhā dhautam nā shreshtham indriyam bhawet

There is no way on the earth to reform a bad man, just as the kidneys cannot become the mouth, a superior part of the body, though washed one hundred times.

11. ॐ

Ātmadweshāt bhawenmrituh pardweshāt dhankshayah

Rājadweshāt bhawenanāsho brahmadweshāt kulkshayah

By offending a kinsman life is lost, by offending others wealth is lost, by offending the king everything is lost, and by offending a Brahmin one's whole family is ruined.

12. ॐ

Varam vanam vyāghragajendrasevitam drumālayam patraphalāmbubhjanam

Trineshu shaiyā shatjeernavalkalam nā bandhumadhye dhanheenajeevanam

It is better to live under a tree in a jungle inhabited by tigers and elephants, to maintain oneself in such a place with ripe fruits and spring water, to lie down on grass and to wear the ragged barks of trees than to live amongst one's relations in utter poverty.

13. ॐ

Bipro brikshastasya mulam cha sandhyā

Vedāhshākhā dharmakarmāni patram

Tasmanmulam yatnato rakshaniyam

Ksheenemule naiva shākhā nā patram

Brahmin is like a tree, his prayers are the roots, his chanting of the Vedas is the branches, and his religious acts are the leaves. Conscious efforts should be taken to preserve the roots, for if the roots are destroyed there can be no branches or leaves.

14. ॐ

Mātā cha Kamalādevi pitādevo Janārdanah

Bandhawā Vishnubhaktāscha swadesho bhuwanatrayam

My mother is Kamaladevi, Goddess Lakshmi, and my father is Lord Janardana Bhagwān Vishnu, and my relatives are the Vishnu *bhaktas*, *Vaishnavas*. Our country possesses all the three worlds.

15. ॐ

Ekbrikshasamārudhā nānā varnā vihangamāh

Prabhāte dashasu dikshu tatra kā parivedana

On a single tree, a great many kinds and number of birds perch throughout the night, but in the morning they fly in all the ten directions. Why should we lament for that?

16. ॐ

Buddhiryasya balatasya nirbuddhestu kuto balam

Vane sinho madonmatattah shashakena nipātitam

He who is intelligent and wise is strong; those who lack wisdom have no strength. The lion moved with pride in the forest but was killed by an intelligent rabbit.

17. ॐ

Kā chintā mam jeevane yadi Harih Viswambharo geeyate

Nā chedarbhakjeevanāya jananiatasya katham nirmayet

Ityālochya muhurmuhuryadupate Laxmipatekevalam

Twatpādāmbujasevanena satatam kālo mayā neeyate

Why should I be worried for my maintenance when Lord Vishwambhara Vishnu supports all? Without the grace of Lord Hari, how could milk flow from a mother's breast for a child's nourishment? By repeatedly thinking like this, O Lord of the Yadus, O husband of Lakshmi, the Master of the three worlds, I spend all my time in serving Your lotus feet.

18. ॐ

Girvānvānishu vishishtha buddhisstathāpi bhāshānteralolupoaham

Yathā surānāmamrite sthteapi swargāngnānāmadharāsave ruchih

I have lust for languages other than Sanskrit, as the gods who reside in heaven and drink the nectar cherish the wish to enjoy the sap of the lips of the heavenly nymphs.

19. ॐ

Annāddashagunam pistam pistāddashgunam payah
Payaso ashtagunam mānsam mānsāddashgunam ghritam

There is ten times more energy in the flour than grain. There is ten times more energy in milk than in flour. There is eight times more energy in meat than in milk. There is ten times more energy in ghee than in meat.

20. ॐ

Shākena roga vardhante payasa vardhante tanuh
Ghritena vardhattam veeryam mānasānmānsam prabardhate

Excess of green vegetables increases the number of diseases, milk helps body to develop, ghee helps semen to form and collect and flesh makes the flesh grow.

Niti – 11

1. ॐ

Dātritwam priyavaktritwaṁ dheeratwamuchitagyatā

Abhyāsena nā labhate chatwārah sahajā gunāh

Generosity in dealing, sweet and pleasing speech, courage and propriety of thinking and conduct are not acquired; these four integral qualities are inborn.

2. ॐ

Ātmavargam parityajya parvargam samāshrayet

Swayameva layam yāti yathā rājānyadharmatah

They who forsake their own community and join another perish as the king who follows different religion, when he fails to protect his subject.

3. ॐ

Hasti sthultanuh sa cha ankushvashah kim hastimātroankusho

Deepe prajwalite pranashyati tamah kim deepmātram tamah

Vajrenāpi hatāh patanti girayah kim vajramātro giram

Tejo yasya virājate sa balwān sthuleshu kah pratayah

The elephant has a huge body but is controlled by a little goad. Is the goad as big as an elephant? A lighted earthen lamp banishes darkness. Is the earthen lamp as vast as the darkness? A mountain is broken even by a thunderbolt. Is the thunderbolt as heavy as the mountain? He who has energy and might is really powerful. Physical appearance has no meaning.

4. ॐ

Kalau dashasahasreshu Haristyajati medinim

Tadartham Juānhwitoyam tadartham grāmdevtā

It is believed that ten thousand years after the onset of *Kaliyug*, the Almighty will forsake the earth. After just half of it, that is, five thousand years, the water of Gangā will evaporate, and after further half of it, that is, two thousand five hundred years, the local god of a village will forsake that village.

It means that ten thousand years after the onset of *Kaliyug*, there will be no God or religion on the earth. It will be complete anarchy. There will be no water in the rivers, people will fight for it; and there will be no godly thing left in a village which will be the end of social semblance and order.

(One can visualise the future in context of the present situation of nuclear race, ozone hole and greenhouse effect.)

5. ॐ

Grihā āsaktasya no vidyā no dayā mānsbhojinah

Dravyalubadhasya no satyam strainasya nā pativratā

He who is deeply involved in family life can never acquire knowledge, there can be no mercy in those who eat flesh, the man who is greedy of money cannot be truthful, and purity and sincerity cannot be found in a woman.

6. ॐ

Nā durjanah sādhudashāmupaiti bahuprakārairapi shikshyamānah

Āmulsiktah payasā ghritena nā nimbabriksho madhuratwameti

As the neem tree will not become sweet even if milk and ghee are pasted from roots to the top, in the same way a wicked cannot become gentle even if he is taught in different ways.

7. ॐ

Untargatamalo dustateerthasnānashatarapi

Nā shudhyati yathā bhāndam surāyā dāhitam cha yat

As a wine pot cannot be purified even by evaporating all the wine by fire, in the same way a dirty mind cannot be purged even when one takes hundred baths in a sacred river.

8. ॐ

Nā veti yo yasya gunaprakarsham

Sa tam sadā nindati nā atra chitram

Yathā kirāti karikumbhajātā

Muktāh parityajya bibharti gunjāh

It is not a wonder when a person reviles a thing about which he has no knowledge, just as a *bhilani* (a woman of hunter tribe) wears the garland of *ghunghachi* (a small red and black seed) in place of wearing the pearl extracted from the head of an elephant.

9. ॐ

Ye tu sambatsaram purnam nityam mounena bhunjate
Yugakotisahasram tu swargaloke mahiyate

He who eats his meals silently for one year lives with honour in heaven for thousands of years.

10. ॐ

Kamam krodham tathā lobham swādam shringārakautuke
Atinidrā atiseve cha vidyārthi hyasta varjayet

A student must renounce the following eight things — sex, anger, greed, delicious dishes, care for beauty, entertainment, excessive sleep, and sycophancy.

11. ॐ

Akrishtaphalmulena vanvāsaratah sadā
Kurute ahrahah shrādhamrishiviprah sa uchayate

That Brahmin is said to be a *rishi* who lives on the fruits and roots grown in uncultivated lands, who always lives in forests happily and acts for the emancipation of the dead and living alike (by performing '*shrādh*' every moment).

12. ॐ

Ekāhārena santushtah shatkarmaniratah sadā
Ritukālāvigāmini cha sa vipro dwija uchayate

He alone is a true Brahmin who is satisfied with one meal a day, performs six duties and cohabits with his wife only once in a month on a day after her menses only for children.

13. ॐ

Loukikekartmani rartah pashunām paripalakah
Vānijyakrishikartā yah sa vipro vaishya uchayate

That Brahmin who is engrossed in worldly affairs, brings up cows and is engaged in trade and agriculture is called a *vaishya*.

14. ॐ

Lākshāditailaneelānām kusumbhamamadhusarpishām
Vikretāmadyamānsānām sa viprah shudra uchayate

The Brahmin who deals in lac-die, articles, oil, indigo, silken cloth, honey, clarified butter, wine, and flesh is called a *shudra*.

15. ॐ

Parkāyavihantā cha dāmbhikah swarthasādhakah
Chhali dweshi mriduh kruro vipro mārjār uchayate

The Brahmin who destroys the doings of others, is hypocritical, selfish, and a deceitful hater, and while speaking mildly, cherishes cruelty at heart, is called a cat.

16. ॐ

Vāpi-kupa-tadāgānāmārāma-sur-veshmanām
Uchchhedane nirā āshankah sa vipro malechha uchayate

The Brahmin who destroys a pond, a well, a tank, a garden and a temple is called a *malechha.*

17. ॐ

Devadrvyam gurudravyam pardārā abhimarshanam
Nirwāhah sarvabhuteshu vipraschāndāla uchayate

The Brahmin who steals the property of the Deities and the gurus, who keeps relation with another's wife and who is omnivorous is called a *chāndāla.*

18. ॐ

Deyam bhojyadhanam sadā sukritibhirno sanchintvyam kadā
Shri Karnasya Baleshcha Vikrampaterdyāpi kritih stithā
Asmākam madhu dānbhogarahitam nastam chiratnachitam
Nirvānāditi pānipādayugale gharshyantyaho makshikāh

In place of accumulating wealth, one should give away in charity that he has in excess of his needs. By only charity, Karna, Bali and King Vikramaditya survive even today. It is so because the accumulated wealth is destroyed like the honey stored by the honeybees which neither enjoy it themselves nor give it in charity, and despair when someone else takes it away from them.

Niti – 12

1. ॐ

Sānandam sadanam sutāscha sudhiyah kāntā priyālāpani

Ikshāpurtidhanam swayoshitiratih swā āgyāparāh sevakāh

Ātithya Shivapujanam pratidinam mistānnapānam grihe

Sādhoh sangamupāsate cha satatam dhanyo grihastāh āshramah

He is a blessed householder (*grihastha*) who lives in his own house in a peaceful atmosphere, whose sons and daughters are wise and gentle, whose beautiful wife speaks sweetly, who is diligent and has enough wealth earned by honest means, whose needs and desires are fulfilled, who finds pleasure in the company of his wife, whose servants are obedient, in whose house hospitality is shown, the Supreme Lord Shiva is worshipped and sweets are eaten every day, and who meditates in the company of saints. Such a householder is great and happy.

2. ॐ

Ārteshu vipreshu dayānwitashcha yat shradhayā swalapamupaiti dānam

Anantapāram samupaiti rājan yadiyate tanna labhed dwijebhyah

One who devotedly gives a little to a Brahmin who is in distress is recompensed abundantly. Hence, O King, what is given to a good Brahmin is got back not in an equal quantity, but in an infinitely higher degree.

3. ॐ

Dākshinatam swajane dayā parjane shāthyam sadā durjane

Preetih sādhujane smayah khalajane dwijajane chārgawam

Shouryam shatrjane kshamā gurujane, nārijane dhrishtatā

Etatham nye purushāh kalāshu kushalāsteswevawaloka stithih

Only he lives happily in this world who deals with his relatives sweetly and gently. He is kind and generous. He deals with the wicked fittingly. He shows love towards the good and respect and sweetness towards the learned. He is shrewd in his dealings with the base, simply and frankly. He is courageous against the enemies, forgiving towards the guru and is tolerant towards women. He does not believe blindly in women but deals with them intelligently. He is an expert. And, the world exists and moves because of such men.

4. ॐ

Hastau dānvivarjitau shrutiputau sāraswatdrohinau

Netre sādhuvilokanena rahite pādau nā teertham gatau

Anyāyārjitavittapurnamunderam garvena tungam shiro

Re re jambuka munch munch sahasā nindyam sunindyam vapuh

He whose hands have given nothing in charity, whose ears have not heard the moral teachings of the scriptures, whose eyes have not beheld a gentle soul and pure devotees of the Lord, whose feet have never travelled to holy places, who never served the gurus and teachers, who lived on the things earned by crooked means and yet holds his head high in vanity, is a jackal in the form of man. He should immediately leave his body. His death is more important than his life.

5. ॐ

Patram naiva yadā kareervitape dosho basantasya kim

Noluko apyawalokate yadi diwā suryasya kim dushanam

Varshā naiva patani chātak mukhe meghasya kim dushnam

Yatpurvam vidhinā lalātlikhitam tanmārjitam kah kshamah

What is the fault of spring that the bamboos have no leaves? What is the fault of the sun if an owl cannot see during the daytime? What is the fault of the clouds if no raindrops fall into the mouth of the *chātak* bird? Who can avoid what has been inscribed upon our foreheads by Brahma at the time of birth?

6. ॐ

Satsangātbhawati hi sādhutā khalānām

Sādhunām nā hi khalsangmātkhaltwam

Āmodam kusum-bhawam mrideva dhatte

Mridgandham nā hi kusumāni dhāryanti

A wicked man may develop saintly qualities in good company of saints, but a devotee does not become wicked in the company of a wicked person as the earth absorbs the scent of a flower but the flowers do not take the odour of the earth.

7. ॐ

Sādhunām darshanam punyam teerthabhutā hi sādhavah

Kālena phalate teertham sadyah sādhusamāgatāh

One indeed becomes blessed by meeting a devoted saint for they are like pilgrimages in themselves. Such devotee saints purify us immediately, whereas the sacred pilgrimages give result only at the appointed hour.

8. ॐ

Viprā asminnagare mahān kathaya? Kastādrumānām ganah

ko dātā? Rajako dadāti vasanam prātargrihitwā nishi

ko dakshah? Pardarvittaharanena sarve api daksho janah

Kasmajivasi he sakhe? Vishakriminyānena jeevāvyām

(This particular *shloka* presents a living picture of the modern society which has become poisonous and hence deadly.)

A stranger asked a Brahmin, "Tell me, who is great in this city?"

The Brahmin replied, "The cluster of *palmyra* trees is great."

Then the traveller asked, "Who is the most charitable person?"

The Brahmin answered, "The washerman is the most charitable who takes the clothes in the morning and gives them back in the evening."

He then asked, "Who is an expert here?"

The Brahmin answered, "Everyone is an expert in robbing others of their wives and wealth."

The man again asked the Brahmin, "How do you live in such a city?"

The Brahmin promptly replied, "As a worm born in poison survives even in the filthiest place, so do I survive here!"

9. ॐ

Viprapāddodakakardamāni nā vedshāstrdhwanigarjitāni

Swāhā-swadhākār-vivarjitāni samshānatulyāni grihāni tāni

The house in which the lotus-like feet of Brahmins are not washed, in which Vedic *mantras* are not loudly chanted, and in which the holy rites of *swāhāh* and *swādhāh* are not pronounced, is like a crematorium.

10. ॐ

Satyam mātā pitā gyānam dharmo bhrātā dayā swasā

Shāntih patni kshamā putrah shedete mam bāndhavāh

Truth is my mother, and knowledge is my father; religious conduct is my brother, and mercy is my friend, peace is my wife, and forgiveness is my son — these six are my kinsmen.

11. ॐ

Anityāni sharirāni vibhawo naiva shāshwatah

Nityam sannihito mrituh kartavyo dharmasangrahah

Our body is perishable, wealth never remains at one place, and death is always nearby. Hence one should act religiously.

12. ॐ

Āmantranotsavā viprā gāwo navtrintsavāh

Patyutsāhyutā nāryah aham krishnaranotasavah

An invitation is like a celebration for a Brahmin. To get new green grass is a cause of celebration for the cows. Increasing passion in their husbands is the cause of celebration for wives and for the devotees increasing love in the feet of Lord Krishna is like a celebration.

13. ॐ

Mātrvat pardāresu pardraveyasu loshthawat

Ātmawat sarvabhuteshu yah pashyati sa panditā

He is a truly wise man (*pandit*) who regards another's wife as his mother, others' wealth as soil, and all other living beings as his own self.

14. ॐ

Dharma tatparatā mukhe madhurata dāne samutsāhtā

Mitre abanchakatā gurou vinayatā chitte gambhiratā

Āchāre shuchitā gune rasikatā shāshtreshu vigyānatā

Rupe sunderatā Shive bhajantā satsweva sandrishyate

We can find the following attributes only in gentle and virtuous men — religious activity, sweet of tongue, an ardent indulgence in charity, guileless dealings with friends, humility towards guru, seriousness at heart, purity in conduct, amorous and refined appreciation of excellence, specialisation in *shastras*, handsomeness in appearance, devotion to Lord Shiva and moral acts.

15. ॐ

Kāshtham kalpataruh sumerurachashchintāmanih prastarah

Suryastivrakarah shashi kshayakarah kshāro hi vārānnidhih

Kāmo nashtatanurbaliditisuto nityam pashuh kāmgaunairtāste

Tulayāmi bho Raghupate kasyopamā deeyate

Kalpataru (the all-fulfilling tree) is but wood, the Sumeru (the mountain of gold) is immovable, *chintamani* (the gem that takes away care and anxiety) is just a stone, the sun is terribly hot, the moon changes and is prone to wane, the boundless ocean is salty, the god of sex has no body, Bali (the son of Aditi, and known for charity) is a demon, and *Kamadhenu* (the all-giving cow) is only an animal. Now, O Ram, the Lord of Raghu dynasty! With whom should I compare you?

16. ॐ

Vinayam rājputrebhyah panditebhyah subhāshitam
Anritam dyutakārevhyah stribhyah shikshet kaitawam

Courtesy should be learnt from a prince, the concise knowledge from pandits (learned men), lying should be learnt from a gambler and deceit from women.

17. ॐ

Anālokya vyayamkartā hyanāthah kalahpriyah
Āturah sarvakshetreshu narah sheeghram vinashayati

The man who spends without thinking about the future, the homeless headworker, one who is weak but quarrelsome, the man who is interested in women from all walks of life is soon ruined.

18. ॐ

Nāhāram chintayet prāgyo dharmekam hi chintayet
Āhāro hi manushyānām janmanā sah jāyate

The wise man is not worried about his food; he anxiously thinks of conscientious deeds. The food for each one is created with the birth.

19. ॐ

Jalbindunipātena kramashah puryate ghatah
Sa hetuh sarvavidyānām dharmasya cha dhanasya cha

As by pouring water drop by drop a pitcher is filled up, in the same way by slow, steady and continuous acquisition one accumulates wealth, grain and knowledge.

20. ॐ

Wayasah parināmeapi yah khalah khal eva sah
Supakwamsi mādhuryam nopayātindravārunam

The man who remains wicked even during old age is really wicked, just like the *Indrāyana* fruit, which remains sour even after becoming fully ripe.

Niti – 13

1. ॐ

Muhuratamapi jeewecha narah shuklena karmanā

Nā kalpamapi kashtena lokadwayavirodhinā

If a man has to live only for a moment, he should do some pious deeds during that small time. Such a life is a great life. But it is useless to live in this world for a *kalp* (lakhs of years) in pain and doing unwholesome deeds.

2. ॐ

Gate shoko nā kartavyo bhabishyam naiva chintayet

Bartamānena kālena pravartante vichakshanah

We should not mourn for what is past, nor should we worry about future. The wise men think of and work according to the present needs and circumstances.

3. ॐ

Swabhāwena hi tushyanti devāh satpurushah pita

Gyātayah snānapānābhyām vākyadānena panditah

Learned men, gentle and generous men and father get easily and naturally pleased. Friends and relatives are pleased with grand hospitality and feasts and the wise men (*pandits*) with only sweet words.

4. ॐ

Aho bāt bichitrāni charitāni mahā ātmanām

Lakshmi trināya manyate tadbhārena namanti cha

Oh, see what a wonder it is! The life, thinking and doings of the great are strange. They treat wealth as insignificant and as light as a straw, yet when they acquire it, they bend under its weight.

5. ॐ

Yasya sneho bhayam tasya sneho dukhasya bhājanam

Snehamulāni dukhāni tāni tyaktwā basetasukham

He who is deeply attached to someone experiences different kinds of fears and sorrow. The root of all grief is attachment. (The greater the attachment the greater is the grief.) So, one should discard attachment and lead a happy life.

6. ॐ

Anagatavidhātā cha pratyutpannamatistayā

Dwāwetau sukhmedhete yadbhabishyo vinashyati

They both lead a happy and successful life who think of future and are ready to cope with whatever comes their way, and those who face any situation wisely and boldly. But those who depend on the fate and wait for the God to take care are ruined and more often completely.

7. ॐ

Rāgyi dharmini ndharmishthā pāpe pāpāh same samah

Rājānammanuvartante yathā rājā tathā prajāh

If the king is religious and virtuous, then the subjects also follow a similar religious and virtuous path. If the king is disinterested, then the subjects also become non-committed, disinterested and inactive. As a king is, so are the subjects. The subjects follow the example of the king.

8. ॐ

Jeewantam mrtawanmanye dehinam dharmavajittam

Mrito dharmrn sanyukto deerghjeevi nā sansha

Though physically alive that man is dead who does not act religiously, who does everything wrong and against the laws, precepts and teachings of nature.

9. ॐ

Dharmārthakāmamokshānām yasya eko nā vidyte

Azāgalstanasyaeva tasya janma nirarthakam

He who has acquired neither virtue, wealth, satisfaction of desires nor salvation, none of the most needed *dharma*, *artha*, *kama*, *moksha*, is dead. His life is totally useless, like the non-milking nipples hanging from the neck of a goat.

10. ॐ

Dahyamānāh sutivrena neechāh par-asho-agninā

Ashaktāstpadam gantum tato nindām prakuvarte

The hearts of base men burn to see others' fame growing, and when they are unable to rise to that fame, they slander.

11. ॐ

Bandhāya vishyā āsaktam muktai nirvishayam manah

Man wvam manushyānām kāranam bandhamokshayoh

Man is a slave to his mind. Because of the mind, man thinks to be either free or bounded. The lust in man for numerous fascinating things and excessive attachment and indulgence into sensual pleasures leads him to bondage, while detachment from them leads to liberation. It is the mind alone that is responsible for bondage or liberation.

12. ॐ

Ipasitam manasah sarvam kasya sampadyate sukham

Daivā āyattam yatah saravam tasmātsantoshamāshrayet

All the desires of human beings cannot be fulfilled as everything is under the Fate. So, man should be content to work and with what one gets.

13. ॐ

Yathā dhenusahasreshu vatso gachchhati mātaram

Tathā yachcha kritam karma kartāramanugachchhati

As a calf recognises and follows its mother even among a thousand cows, in the same way all the good and bad deeds of a man follow him.

14. ॐ

Dehābhimāne galite vigyāte paramātmani

Yatra yatra mano yāti tatra tatra samādhayah

The body and the mind are two separate entities. When a man learns this difference then his pride regarding his body vanishes. That end of ego is the realisation of God and indulgence into meditation (*samādhi*).

15. ॐ

Unawasthitakāryasya nā jane nā vane sukham

Jane dahati sansargo vane sangvivarjanam

There is no happiness either in the midst of human beings or away from them in a jungle if one's actions are unorganised. In the society, the heart burns at the prosperity of others and in the forest by loneliness.

16. ॐ

Yathā khātwā khanitrena bhutale wāri vindati
Tathā gurugatām vidyām shushrushuradhigachchhati

When one digs the land with a shovel, one gets the underground water. In the same way, a student acquires knowledge by serving his guru, the preceptor.

17. ॐ

Karmāyattam phalam pundām buddhih karmānusārini
Tathāpi sudhiyaschā āryāh suvichāraiva kurvate

Men get the fruits according to their deeds and their deeds are controlled and guided by their action, still the wise and the gentle think well and then act.

18. ॐ

Ekāksherpradātāram yo gurum nābhivandati
Shwānyonishatam bhuktwa chāndāleshwabhijāyate

Even if one has taught the spiritual significance of just one letter, he should be treated and worshipped as a teacher. He, who does not give reverence to such a guru, is born as a dog a hundred times, and then takes birth as a *chāndāla*.

19. ॐ

Yugānte prachalante Meru kalpānte sapta sāgarāh

Sādhavah pratipannārthān nā chalanti kadāchan

At the end of the *yuga*, Mount Sumeru may be displaced, at the end of the *kalpa*, the waters of the seven oceans may be disturbed, but a *sadhu*, a pure devotee, will never leave the work in hand and deviate from the spiritual path.

Niti – 14

1. ॐ

Ātmāparādhabrikshasya phalānyetāni dehinām
Dāridryarogadukhāni bandhanvyasanāni cha

Poverty, disease, sorrow, bondage and other evils are the fruits borne by the tree of one's own sins. One reaps what one sows.

2. ॐ

Panarvittam punarmitram punarbhārya punarmahi
Atatsarvam purnalabhyam nā shariram punah punah

Wealth, a friend, a wife, and a kingdom or land may be acquired again or regained, but one can never get this body (and the mind in it) again.

3. ॐ

Bahunām chaiva sattwānām samawāyo ripunjayah
Varshadhārādharo meghastrinairapi niwāryate

The enemy can be overcome by a union of a large number of people, just as grass collectively stops the flow of fast current or heavy rainfall.

4. ॐ

Jale tailam khale guhyam pātre dānam manāgapi
Prāgye shāstram swayam yāti vistāram vastushaktitah

Oil on water, a secret communicated to a base man, a gift given to a worthy person, and scriptural teaching to learned men when completed, spread out by virtue of their inner nature and power.

5. ॐ

Dharmā ākhyāne shashāne cha roginām yā matirbhawet
Sā sarvadaiva tishthechchet ko nā mucheta bandhanāt

If men should always retain the state of mind they experience when hearing religious instructions, when present at a crematorium ground, and when in sickness, then who could not attain liberation.

6. ॐ

Uttapannapāshchāttāpasya buddhirbhawati yādrishi
Tādrishi yadi purvam shyāt kasya nā syānmahodayah

If the feeling of repentance that we feel after a crime comes before committing the crime, then man can attain liberation.

7. ॐ

Dāne tapasi shaurye wā vigyāne vinaye naye
Vismayo nā hi kartavyo bahuratnā vasundharā

We should not feel pride that we are the best or greatest in our charity, austerity, valour, spiritual knowledge, modesty and moral, for the earth is full of the rare gems.

8. ॐ

Durasthoapi nā durastho yo yasya manasi sthitah
Yo yasya hridaye nāsti samipastoapi duratah

Though one may actually be far away but if he lives in our heart then is very close. But if one is not in our heart, then he is very far away from us though may be living in close vicinity.

9. ॐ

Yasya chāpriyamichchheta tasya bruyāt sadā priyam
Vyādho mrigvadham kartum geetam gāyati suswaram

Talk sweetly to whom you wish to bring harm as the hunter sings sweetly before catching a deer.

10. ॐ

Atyāsannā vināshāya durashthā nā phalpradā
Sevityam madhyabhāgena rājā wanhirguruh striyah

Closeness to a king, fire, guru or a woman completely annihilates, while aloofness from them does not bear fruit, so use them from the middle.

11. ॐ

Agnirāpah striyo murkhāh sarpā rājkulāni cha
Nityam yatnena sevyāni sadyah prānaharāni shat

We should always and every day cautiously deal with fire, water, women, fools, serpents, and members of a royal family, for they can kill us within no time.

12. ॐ

Sa jeevati gunā yasya yasya dharmah sa jeevati
Gundharmabihinasya jeevitam nisprayojanam

Only he should be treated as living that has qualities, is virtuous, pious and religious. Their life is meaningless, who are neither religious nor have virtues.

13. ॐ

Yadichchhasi vashikartum jagadekena karmanā
Parāpvādasasyebhyo gām charanti niwārayam

If you wish to gain control over the world by performing only one deed, then control your tongue (senses) and do not speak ill of any one.

14. ॐ

Prastāvasadrissham vākyam prabhāvasadrisham priyam
Ātmashaktishamam kopam yo jānāti sa panditah

He is a learned man (pandit) who speaks what is suitable to the occasion, renders loving service according to his ability and knows the extreme limit of his anger.

15. ॐ

Eka yewam padārthastu tridhā vhawati vikshitah
Kunapah kāmini mānsam yogibhih kāmibhih swabhih

Though a woman is a single object but she appears as three different things to different figures, she appears as a corpse to the one who practises austerity, to the sensual she is a woman, and to the dogs only a lump of flesh.

16. ॐ

Susiddhamaushdham dharmam grihachchidram
cha maithunam
Kubhuktam kushrutam chaiva matimānna prakāshyet

A wise man should not divulge the formula of a useful medicine, an act of charity, domestic conflicts, sexual enjoyment, tasteless food or an abuse.

17. ॐ

Tāvanmounena neeyante kokilashchaiva wāsarāh
Yāvatsarvajanānandadāyani vākprvartate

The cuckoos remain silent for several seasons until they are able to sing sweetly during the spring season so as to give pleasure to all.

18. ॐ

Dharmam dhanam cha dhānyam cha
gururvachanamoushadham
Sugrihitam cha kartyavyamanyathā tu nā jeevati

It is difficult to lead a good and healthy life otherwise, so we should act religiously, earn and save wealth and grain, follow the words of our spiritual preceptor, and keep medicines well.

19. ॐ

Tyaj durjanasansargam bhaj sādhusamāgamam
Kuru punyamahorātram smar nityamanityatām

Leave the company of the wicked, attend the congregations of saintly persons, do good and collect blessings day and night and remember every day that life is only temporary.

Niti – 15

1. ॐ

Yasyachittam dravibhuttam kripayā sarvajantushu

Tasya gyānena mokshanena kim jatābhasmalepena

If one has real compassion for all living beings, then what has he to do with knowledge, liberation, matted hair or smearing ashes by becoming a *sādhu*?

2. ॐ

Ekamewāksharam yastu guruh shishyam prabodhayet

Prithivyām nāsti taddravyamm yaddtwā cha ānrini bhawet

There is no treasure on earth by giving which a disciple can be free from the debt of that guru who has taught him one word (*akshar*) AUM who is the supreme God.

3. ॐ

Khalānām kantakānām cha dwibidhaiva pratikriyā

Upānanmukhabhango wā durato wā visarjanam

There are two ways to get rid of thorns and wicked persons, either by smashing their mouth with a shoe or by keeping oneself away from them.

4. ॐ

Kuchailinam dantamalopasristam

Bahyashinam nishthurabhāshinim

Suryodaye chāstamite shayānam

Mumunchi shriyadi Chakrapānih

One, who wears dirty clothes, has dirty teeth, is gluttonous, speaks unkindly and sleeps at the sunrise and the sunset, loses wealth, health, beauty and grace, even if he is the Lord Vishnu.

5. ॐ

Tyajanti mitrāni dhanairvihinam

Dārāshcha bhrityāshcha suhridajanāshcha

Tam charthawantam punarāshrayante

Artho hi loke purushasya bandhu

One is forsaken by friends, wife, servants and relatives when he loses his wealth but when he regains his wealth, they all return who had earlier forsaken him. In fact, wealth is a man's real relative.

6. ॐ

Anyāyopārjitam dravyam dash varshāni tishthati
Prāpte cha ekādashe varshe samulam tad vinshyati

Sinfully acquired wealth sustains for only ten years, during the eleventh year, it is destroyed along with the original sum.

7. ॐ

Ayuktam swāminoyuktam yuktam neechasya dushanam
Amritam rāhawe mrituvisham Shankarbhushanam

Something, not in keeping with his power and popularity, done by a powerful person, becomes the reason of his fame but the same thing done by a weak person will be censored by all. The best example is Rahu who was killed when he drank *amrit*. But by taking poison knowingly Bhagwān Shankar came to be known as *Neelkantha*.

8. ॐ

Tadbhojanam yad dwijabhuktashesham
Tatsouhridam yatkriyate parasmin
Sā prāgyatā yā nā karoti pāpam
Dambham binā yeh kryate sa dharmah

A real meal is that which is taken after feeding Brahmins, that love is real which is for others, true wisdom is to remain away from sins and genuine religion is that which is done without ego and without expectations.

9. ॐ

Manirlunthati pādāgre kāchah shirashi dhāryate

Krayvikraybelāyām kāchah kācho manirmanih

Under certain circumstances, the most precious jewel may lie in the dust at the feet, while glass may be worn on the head. But when one goes to buy or sell them, a jewel shows its price and glass its own.

10. ॐ

Anantshastram bahulānshcha vidyāh

Alpascha kālo bahubighnatā cha

Yatsārbhutam tadupāsniyam

Hanso yathā ksheeramiwambumadhyāt

Knowledge of the *shāstras* is unlimited, there are many arts to be learnt, life is limited and there are many obstacles. Naturally, therefore, we must opt for learning and doing. We must learn to distinguish just as a swan takes only the milk and leaves the water mixed in it.

11. ॐ

Durāgatam pathi shrāntam brithā cha grihamāgatam

Anarchayitwā yo bhungakte sa wai chāndāla uchyate

He is taken as an untouchable, sinful person (*chāndāla*) who eats his dinner without feeding the stranger who has accidentally come to his house after travelling quite a long distance.

12. ॐ

Pathanti chaturo vedān dharmashāshtānyanekashah

Ātmānam naiva cha jānanti darvi pākarasam yathā

Though one may have read all the Vedas and scriptures, but he who has not realised his own self is like a ladle which touches and stirs everything in the kitchen but knows the taste of none.

13. ॐ

Dhanyā dwijamayee naukā viparitā bhawārnave

Tarantyadhogatāh sarve upasthitāh patantayadhah

Those are blessed souls who have a strange boat in the form of a Brahmin. It is a strange boat because those who take shelter under it cross over the sea of life but those who sit on them are drowned.

14. ॐ

Ayamamritanidhānam nāyako apyāshadhinām

Amritashareerah kāntiyuktoapi chandrah

Bhawati bigatrashmirmandam prāpya bhānoh

Parsadananiwishtah ko laghutwam nā yāti

He becomes the most ordinary person who goes to live (takes shelter) in another one's house as the moon loses its grace and light when he goes in the sun's house and comes under the influence of the sun.

15. ॐ

Alirayam nalinidalamadhyagah
kamalinimakarandamadālasah

Vidhivshātpardeshamupāgatah kutajpushparasam
bahu manyate

The large black bee resides usually among the lotus flowers with soft petals and drinks sweet nectar to its heart's desire. But when it flies up to alien-looking flowers like *kutaja*, it gets little sap and a lot of pricks from the thorns.

16. ॐ

Peetah kruddhena tātashcharantalhato ballabho yena roshād

Ābālyādwipravayairah swavadanviware dhāryate vairini mey

Geham mey chhedayanti pratidiwasam
Umākāntapujānimittam

Tasmātkhinna sadāham dwijakulnilayam
nāthyuktam tyajāmi

"Why are you angry with the Brahmins? Why don't you live in their house?" Once, Lord Visnu asked His spouse Lakshmi in this way.

Lakshmi replied, "O Lord, Agastya *rishi* drank up my father (the ocean) in a fit of anger; Bhrigu *rishi* kicked you in anger; Brahmins have pride over themselves and worship my competitor Saraswati, and they pluck each day the lotus flowers which are my abode, and they worship Lord Shiva. Therefore, O Lord, I have left their abode."

17. ॐ

Bandhanāni khalu santi bahuni
premarajjudridhabandhanamanyat

Dāruvedanipunoapi shadamghrirnishkriyo
bhawati pankajakoshe

There are different knots in this world but the knot of love is very strange. The black bee which can pierce wood prefers to remain a captive throughout the night when caught inside lotus flowers but it never tries to cut the petals and come out.

18. ॐ

Chhinnoapi chandanatarurna jahāti gandham
Briddhoapi vāranapatirna jahāti leelām
Yantrārpito madhuratām nā jahāti chekshuh
Ksheenoapi nā tyajati sheelgunān kuleenam

Even when cut into pieces the sandalwood retains its fragrance, even when old an elephant behaves in its natural way, although sugarcane is crushed in a mill it does not forsake its sweetness, in the same way a man from a refined and cultured community always behaves in the most human way.

Niti – 16

1. ॐ

Nā dhyātam padamishwaraya vidhivatsamsārvichchhattaye
Swarg dwār kapāta pātana paturthamoapi nopārjitah
Nāripina payodharuyugalam swapneapi nāligitam
Mātuh kewalmeva yauvanvanchchhede kuthārā vayam

They work as an axe to cut down their mother's tree of youthfulness who do not meditate over the form of the Almighty to get free from the net of the world, who do not collect the wealth of meritorious deeds to open the door of heaven and who do not hug the well-built breast and thighs of a woman.

2. ॐ

Jalpanti sārdhamanyena pashyantyanyam sabibhramāh
Hridaye chintayantyanyam nā strināmekato ratih

He is a fool who thinks that some prostitute loves him, for women do not love only one person. When she is talking to one, she may be communicating with another with her action and she may be thinking of a third one in her heart. It is their nature.

3. ॐ

Yo mohānmanyate mudho rakteyam mayi kāmini
Sa tasya bashgo bhutwā nritayet krirā-shakuntawat

He is a fool who thinks that a charming young dame loves him. He becomes her prey and slave and dances like a *shakunt* bird.

4. ॐ

Koarthān prāpya nā garbito bishayinah kasyāpadoastam gatāh
Stribhih kasya nā khanditam bhuvi manah ko nām rāgyām priyah
Kah kālasya nā gocharatwamagamatkoarthi gato gauravam
Ko wā durjawāgurāsu patitah kshemena yātah pathi

Who is there who does not feel pride after becoming rich? Who is there who does not suffer after becoming licentious? Who is there who does not fall prey to a beautiful young lady? Who is there who has always been loved by the king? Who is there who has not been beaten by time? What beggar has attained glory? Who has lived happily after coming in contact with the wicked?

5. ॐ

Nā nirmitah kena nā drishtapurvah nā shruyate hemamayah kurangah
Tathāpi trishnā Raghunandansya bināshkāle biparit buddhih

Up till now there has not been a golden deer nor has it been seen by anyone, yet Sri Ram felt impassioned to catch such a deer made up of gold. It is true that when destruction knocks at the door, a person starts thinking in the opposite direction.

6. ॐ

Gunairuttamatām yāti nochchairāsansansthitāh
Prasādshikharastoapi kākah kim garudāyate

A man attains greatness by his merits, not simply by occupying a high position. Can a crow be called a *garuda* (a mythical bird which is a vehicle of Lord Vishnu) simply because he is sitting at the top of a palace?

7. ॐ

Gunāh sarvartra pujayante nā mahatyoapi sampadah
Purnendu kim tathā vandyo nishkalanko yathā krishah

A man gets respect only with his inner qualities and not by his wealth. A small but bright and spotless new moon of the second day gets more respect than the spotted full moon.

8. ॐ

Par-proktaguno yastu nirgunoapi guni bhawet
Indroapilaghutām yāti swayam prakhyāpitairgunaih

The man who is praised by others as great is regarded as worthy though really devoid of those merits. But the man who praises his own qualities is lowered in the estimation of others though he may be Indra, the god of heaven.

9. ॐ

Vivekinamanuprāptā gunā yānti manogyatām
Sutarām ratnamābhāti chāmikarniyojitam

A jewel embedded in a golden ornament becomes more attractive, so a man should try to keep on adding some qualities in his personality wisely, consciously and diligently.

10. ॐ

Gunaih sarvagyatulyoapi sidyatyekonirāshrayah
Unarghyamapi mānikyam hemāshrayamapekshate

A man with the qualities of knowing everything but without a shelter feels pain and is aggrieved like a jewel, which wishes to be embedded in a golden ornament.

11. ॐ

Yatikleshena ye chārthā dharmasyātikramena tu
Shatrunām pranipātena te hyārthā mā bhawantu mey

I would not take that wealth which is snatched from others after inflicting injury and giving pain, which has been accumulated through unwholesome deeds, which has been given by the enemy in lieu of surrender and flattery.

12. ॐ

Kim tayā kryate lakshmyā yā badhuriva kevalā
Yā tu veshyeva sā mānyā pathikairapi bhujyate

The wealth, which is like a married lady for the use of a single person, is meaningless. That wealth is really useful, which is spent on public welfare.

13. ॐ

Dhaneshu jeevitavyeshu strishu chāhārkarmasu
Atriptāh prāninah sarve yātā yāsyanti yānti cha

There is no one in the world who has felt satisfied after making different uses of money and wealth. None feel satiated with the enjoyment of wealth and women. They even pass away discontented and unsatisfied.

14. ॐ

Ksheeyante sarvadānāni yagyahomebalikriyāh

Nā ksheeyate pātradānambhayam sarvadehinām

All charities and sacrifices and all types of *yajnas* are destroyed, only the charity given to a deserving person and the security offered to the living beings remain for ever.

15. ॐ

Trinam laghu trintulam tulādapi cha yāchakah

Vāyunām kim nā nitoasau māmayam yāchayisyati

A blade of grass is very light, much lighter than cotton, and the beggar is lighter still. Why does not the wind carry him away? Because it fears that he may ask alms from him. One must note here that one who asks for alms falls in the eyes of all and becomes lighter than a blade of grass.

16. ॐ

Varam prānparityāgo mānbhangena jeevanāt

Prāntyāge kshanam dukham mānbhange dine dine

It is better to die than to lead a life of disgrace. The loss of life causes but grief for a moment, while disgrace brings pain and grief every day.

17. ॐ

Priyvākyapradānena sarve tushyanti jantawah

Tasmātadeva vaktavyam vachane kā daridratā

All creatures are pleased by sweet tongue and loving words, therefore, we should always speak sweetly to please all. One should never be bankrupt of sweet words.

18. ॐ

Samsārvishbrikshasya dwe phale amritopame
Subhāshitam cha suswādu sangati sujane jane

On the poisonous tree of the world, there are two nectar-like fruits — one is eloquently spoken universal truth (*subhāshita*) and the other is good company of saint.

19. ॐ

Janma janmanyabhyastam dānamadhyayanam tapah
Tenaivā abhyāsyogena tadevābhyasyate punah

One should honestly try to do something good for life and humanity. The practice of charity, learning and meditation in different past lives creates a habit of doing those things in this life too. If we do good to others, we will carry that habit into our next life.

20. ॐ

Pustakeshu yathā vidyā parhastagatam yaddhanam
Utapanneshu cha karyeshu nā sā vidyā nā taddhanam

If one's knowledge lies in books and not in mind or life and if one's wealth is in the possession of others, it can not be helpful or utilised when needed most. Such knowledge or wealth is of no use.

Niti – 17

1. ॐ

Pustakpratayayādhitam nādhitam gurusannidhau

Sabhāmadhye nā sobhante jārgarbhāeva striyah

Those who have acquired knowledge only through books and not under the guidance of a competent teacher cannot shine in an assembly as a woman with an illegal pregnancy is not honoured in the society.

2. ॐ

Krite pratikritam kuryād hinsane pratihinsanam

Tatra dosho nā patati duste dustam samācharet

One should pay others in the same coin, be humble with those who are humble and meet violent with violence. There is no sin to be wicked to a wicked person.

3. ॐ

Yadduram yaddurārādhyam yachcha dure vyavasthitam

Tatsarvam tapasā sādhyam tapo hi duratikramam

Nothing is beyond the reach of spiritual austerity and meditation. The things, which are away from us or impossible to get or beyond our reach, can be accomplished by it (*tapasyā*).

4. ॐ

Lobhaschedagunena kim pishunatā yadyasti kim pātakai
Satyam chattapasā cha kim shuchi mano yadasti teerthena kim
Saujanyam yadi kim gunaih sumahimā yadyasti kim mandanaih
Sadvidyā yadi kim dhanairpayasho yadyasti kim mrituna

One needs no other vice if he has lust. No other sin is required if one practises slander. If one is truthful, then he needs no austerity. If one has a pure heart, then he needs not go for pilgrimages. One needs no other virtue if one has a good disposition. If a man's fame is spreading, he needs no other ornament. If one has great knowledge, then he needs no wealth. If a man's notoriety is growing and he is getting no respect, then he is dead, though alive.

5. ॐ

Pitā ratnākaro yasya laxmiryasya sahodarā
Shankho bhikshātanam kuryānnādattamupatishthate

The conch (*shankh*) is the son of sea, which has all the jewels and thus he is a brother of Lakshmi, the goddess of wealth. Yet, it moves from house to house in the hands of pandits and beggars for charity and alms. It has nothing of its own, for it has not given something as charity.

6. ॐ

Ashaktastu bhawetsādhurbrahmachāri cha nirdhanah
Vyādhistho devabhaktashcha vridhā nāri pativratā

When there is no way out, then people change. This change is not their natural and genuine character. A weak man becomes a saint, a man without wealth prefers to live as *brahmachari*, without marriage, a sick man becomes a devotee of the lord and an old woman turns to be honest and sincere to her husband.

7. ॐ

Nā annodakasamam dānam nā tithi dwādashi samā

Nā gāyatrayāh paro mantro nā mātuh param daivatam

The charity of grain and water is incomparable, there is no day equal to the twelfth day of the moon, there is no mantra greater than Gayatri Mantra, and there is none higher than the mother. She holds a higher status than the gods, for she gives us birth.

8. ॐ

Takshasya visham dante makshikāstu mastake

Vrishchikasya visham puchchhe sarvānge durjane visham

The poison of a serpent is in its fangs, that of a fly in the mouth, and in the tail (sting) of a scorpion, but there is poison in every part of a wicked man.

9. ॐ

Patyurāgyā binā nāri uposhya vratchārini

Āyushyam harate bhartuh sā nāri narakam vrajet

The woman who fasts and observes religious rituals without the permission of her husband shortens his life, and goes to hell and faces great agony.

10. ॐ

Nā dāne shudhyati nāri nopawāsashatairapi

Nā teertha sevayā tadvad bhatuh pādodakairyathā

A woman does not get as purified by charity or by observing hundreds of fasts, or by serving at the places of pilgrimage, as by sipping the water used to wash her husband's feet, that is, by serving her husband.

11. ॐ

Dānena pānirna tu kankanena snānena shuddhirna tu chandanena

Mānena triptirna tu bhojanena gyānena muktirna tu mandanena

The hands are adorned not by ornaments but by charity, the body gets cleaned not by smearing sandal but by bathing, hunger is satiated not by food but by respect, and salvation is not attained by self-adornment but by acquiring spiritual knowledge.

12. ॐ

Nāpitasya grihe kshouram pāshāne gandhlepanam

Ātmarupam jale pashyan shakrashyāpi shriyam haret

One loses his dignity by going to a barber for shaving, by smearing sandal on stones and by looking one's image in water.

13. ॐ

Sadyah pragyāharā tundi sadyah pragyākari vachā

Sadyah shaktiharā nāri sadyah shaktikaram payah

By eating *tundi* one loses intelligence, but by eating *vacha* one regains power in mental faculty; a woman immediately takes away the energy, while milk restores it.

14. ॐ

Paropakaranam yeshām jāgarti hridaye satām

Nasyanti vipadasteshām sampadah syuh pade pade

He who nurtures benevolence at his heart overcomes all difficulties and gets all types of riches at every step.

15. ॐ

Āhārnidrābhayamaithunamcha sāmānyametat pashubhirnarānām

Dharmehiteshāmdhiko vishesho dharmena hināh pashubhih samānāh

Men have eating, sleeping, fearing and mating in common with the animals. Man excels the beasts in reasoning and knowledge, hence, indiscreet men without knowledge are beasts.

16. ॐ

Dānārthino madhukarā yadi karnatālair

Durikritāh karivarena madāndhabuddhayā

Tasyaiva gandayugamandanhānireshā

Bhringāh punarvikachapadmavane basanti

If a proud elephant drives out by fanning his ears the bees that seek the liquid oozing from his head, it is certainly a loss to the elephant and not the bees who feel satisfied with the juice that they get from the lotus.

17. ॐ

Rājā veshyā yamo hyagnistaskaro bāllvchakau

Pardukham nā jānanti ashtamo grāmkantakah

The following eight are like tax collectors and they do not feel the pain and suffering of the people — a king, a prostitute, Yamarāja, a thief, children, beggars, fire and suckers of villagers.

18. ॐ

Adhah pashyasi kim briddhe patitam tava kim bhuvi

Re re murkha nā jānāsi gatam tārunyamoutikam

(Someone asks a lady) "O lady, why are you looking downward? Have you lost something? Has something fallen on the ground?"

(She replies) "O fool, don't you see I have lost the pearl of my youth?"

19. ॐ

Vyālāshrayā api biphalāpi sakantakā api

Vakrā api pankil bhawā api durāsadā api

Gandhena bandhurasi ketaki sarvajantor

Ekoh gunah khalu nihanti samastadoshān

O *ketaki* flower! Serpents live with you, you bear no fruits, your have thorns, you have no speciality, you thrive in mud, and you are not easily accessible. Still for your exceptional fragrance, you are as dear as kinsmen to others. Hence, a single excellence overcomes a multitude of blemishes.

SECTION – III

Niti Shastra

Niti Shastra

Namah shukrabrihaspatibhyām = I salute the teacher of demons, Shukracharya, and the teacher of the gods, Acharya Brihaspati.

Sukhasya mulam dharmah = Religion is the basis of happiness.

Dharmasya mulam artham = Economy is the basis of religion.

Arthasya mulam rājyam = Kingdom is the basis of economy.

Rājyamulamindriyajayah = Control over senses is the basis of kingdom.

Indriyajayasya mulam vinayam = Humility is the basis of control over the senses.

Vinayasya mulam vridhopasevā = Fostering the old is the basis of humility.

Vridhopasyevayā vigyānam = Fostering the old is wisdom.

Vigyānenātmānam sampādayet = Wisdom makes every work possible.

Sampāditātmā jitātmā bhawati = He is a winner who accomplishes all.

Jitātmā sarvārthaih sanyujyet = He possesses all who has won the self.

Arthasampat prakritisampadam karoti = The economy enriches with the natural wealth.

Prakriti sampadā hyanāyakamapi rājyam niyate = With natural wealth, a kingdom can run well without a leader.

Prakritikopah sarvakopebhyo gariyān = The anger of Nature is more destructive than anyone else's.

Abinitaswāmilābhādaswāmilābhah shreyān = In absence of a gentle master, it is better to be without a master.

Sampādyātmānamanwichchet sahāyawān = A king must possess royal nature and should keep similar assistants to govern.

Nāsahāyasya mantranischayah = Without able assistants, a king cannot be sure of his stance.

Naikam chakram paribhramayati = One wheel cannot keep the vehicle (kingdom) moving.

Sahāyah samadukhasukhah = He is the best assistant who behaves equally well both in prosperity and adversity.

Māni pratimāninamātmani dwitiyam mantramutpādayet = During a crisis, a king should keep favouable and adverse ideas in view and take decision after thinking over them.

Abinitam snehamātrena nā mantre kurvita = A man without truth and conscience cannot assist only because he is in favour.

Shrutavantamupadhāshuddham mantrinam kuryāt = Only he should be appointed a minister who has been secretly tested and possesses logic, judgement and ability to give advice.

Mantamulāh sarvārambhāh = One should start a work only after adequate planning.

Mantrarakshane karyasiddhih bhawati = Success comes only by keeping the planning secret.

Mantravisrāvi karyam nāshyati = The effort is doomed if the planning is not kept secret.

Pramadād dwishatām vashamupayāsyati = A momentary lapse will make the secret out, which will crucify one by helping the enemy.

Sarvadwārebhyo mantro rakshitabyah = All the ways of leakage of the secret must be guarded well.

Mantra sampadā hi rājyam vardhate = The prosperity of a kingdom depends on keeping the planning secret.

Shreshthatamām mantraguptimāhuh = The doctrine to keep the thinking secret is the best doctrine.

Kāryāndhasya pradeepo mantrah = The planning is like the light that shows the path under darkness.

Mantrachakshushā parchhidrānyawalokayanti = The conscious king who hopes to win reads the weaknesses of his opponent from the eyes of his ministers.

Mantrakāle nā matsarah kartavyah = No joke while in conference.

Trayānāmekavākye sampratyayah = Decisions should be taken unanimously.

Kāryākāryatatwārthadarshino mantranāh = Only they should be the ministers who understand well what should be pursued, who do not wish for more salary and who know the value of the secrecy of advice and planning.

Shatkarnād bhidyate mantrah = Whatever goes to six ears will not remain a secret.

Āpatsu snehasanyukatam mitram = During a crisis, when a person is left alone, the man who comes forward to help him is a friend.

Mitrasangrahane balam sampadayate = His power increases who collects and keeps many friends.

Balwāna labdhalābhe pryatate = With the power of true friends, one should try to fulfil the wishes (to accumulate wealth or conquer others).

Alabdhalābho nālasasya = A lazy person cannot achieve great heights.

Alasasya labdhamapi rakshitum nā shakyate = A lazy person cannot protect what has already been acquired.

Nā chālasasya rakshitam vivardhate = A lazy person cannot protect what has been gifted to him.

Nā bhrityān preshayati = A lazy king or officer cannot get maximum advantage from the employees.

Alabdhalābhādi chatustayam rājyatantram = The following are the four fundamental works of a kingdom: (i) To achieve which has not been achieved as yet, (ii) To protect what has already been achieved, (iii) To add to the achievements, and (iv) To righteously and wisely appoint the government servants.

Rājyatantrāyatam nitishāstram = A king should follow the doctrine popular among the people.

Rājyatantreshwāyatau tantrāwāpau = The defined works and duties regarding one's own and other countries are important parts of governance.

Tantram swavishayakrityeshwāyattam = Internal management is a system, which is confined to one's own country.

Āwāpo mandalaniwishtah = The dealings with other countries is confined to other countries.

Sandhivigrahyonirmandatah = The treaties and other managements are important aspects of relations with neighbouring countries.

Nitishāshtrānugo rājā = A king should follow moral principles.

Anantarprakritih shatruh = Everything unnatural is an enemy.

Ekāntaritam mitramishyate = Friendship should be extended to an enemy of an enemy.

Hetutah shatru mitre bhavishyatah = There is a reason behind friendship or enmity.

Heeyamānah sandhim kurvita = A weak king should enter into treaty.

Tejo hi sandhānhetustadarthānām = The treaties can be durable and profitable only when both the kings follow dictates equally well.

Nātaptaloho lohena sandhiyate = As hot iron mixes with hot iron, in the same way a treaty succeeds when both the kings are powerful.

Balwān heenena vigrahiyāt = A powerful king should attack only a weak king.

Nā jyāyasā samena wā = One should not grow enmity with equally or more powerful.

Gajpādavigrahmiva balavadwigrahah = To wage war against a powerful king is like getting an infantry smashed under the huge feet of elephants.

Āmapātramāmena sah vinashayati = Two equally powerful kings are destroyed in war as two raw pitchers break down when hit by one another.

Ariprayatanamabhisamikshet = A king should critically analyse the moves made by the enemy kings.

Sandhāyaikato wā = For success, a king should keep an eye on the activities of another king under treaty or without a treaty.

Arivirodhādātmarakshāmāwaset = A king should protect the kingdom against internal and external conspiracies.

Shaktiheeno balwantamāshrayet = A weak king should grow friendship with a strong king.

Durbalāshrayo dukhamāwahati = The shelter of a weak king is painful.

Agnivadrājānamāshrayeṭ = After breaking relation, one should be alert from that king as one dreads the fire.

Rāgyah pratikulam nācharet = One should not go against a king.

Uddhatveshadharo nā bhawet = One should not wear such clothes, which show arrogance or rudeness.

Nā dyevacharitam charet = One should not copy the life and character of a king.

Dwayorapirshyatoh dwaidhibhāwam kurvita = One should create differences between two persons who are jealous of the king (to nip the bud of conspiracy).

Nā vyasanparasya kāryāwāptih = A man fallen in bad habits can never succeed.

Indriyavashavarti chaturangawānapi vinashayati = The king with all the four great forces is destroyed when under the control of the senses.

Nāsti kāryam dyutapravritasya = Gamblers cannot perform their duties.

Mrigayāparasya dharmārthau vinashayatah = Excessive indulgence in hunting keeps a king away from duty and thus destroys the wealth.

Arthaishanā nā vyasaneshu ganyate = To work in order to accumulate wealth for safe and good living is not included in addiction.

Nā kāmāsakatasya kāryānushthānam = Excessive indulgence in sex results in non-functioning.

Agni dāhādapi vishishtam wākpārushyam = Rude words burn more than fire.

Dandapārushyāt sarbjandweshyo bhawati = A judge becomes the enemy of all when he delivers the judgement under prejudice or enmity.

Arthatoshinam shrih parityajati = The king who feels satisfied with little wealth is relinquished by Goddess Lakshmi.

Amitro dandanityāmāyattah = The degree of the success of an enemy depends on one's own power to punish.

Dandanitim adhistishthan prajāh sanrakshati = He saves his countrymen who keeps the power to punish.

Dandah sampadām yojayati = The power to punish adds to the wealth.

Dandbhāwe mantrivargābhāwah = In the absence of a strong system of judgement, the king falls in the grip of weak and selfish ministers and sycophants.

Nā dandādakaryāni kurvanti = Criminals keep themselves away from conspiracy against a king out of the fear of punishment.

Dandanityāmāyatamātmarakshanam = One can be saved by strong rules.

Ātamani rakshite sarve rakshitam bhawati = A king's security guarantees the security of the people.

Ātmāyatau briddhivināshau = A man's prosperity and annihilation are under his control.

Dando hi vigyāne praniyate = The rules should be applied wisely.

Darbaloapi rājā nāwamantabyah = One should not think a king to be weak so to disobey him.

Nāstyagnerdaurbalyam = Fire should never be taken as weak.

Dande pratiyate britih = The administrative ability of a king is projected by his power to punish.

Vritimulamarthalābhah = The prosperity of a kingdom depends on the character of the king.

Arthamulau dharmakāmau = The wealth of a kingdom depends on dutifulness, religiosity and action of its subjects.

Arthamulam kāryam = The wealth keeps one active.

Yadalpaprayatnāt kāryasidhirbhawati = With wealth at hand, works are completed easily.

Upāyapurvam nā duskaram syāt = The work is completed when done scientifically under a planning.

Anupāyapurvam kāryam kritamapi vinashayati = A work is abandoned unfinished when started without planning.

Kāryārthināmupāya yeva sahāyah = Planning and work culture are strong helping stairs.

Kāryam purushakārena lakshyam sampadyate = A work with all its features known becomes a goal.

Purushkāramanuvatate daivam = Fate follows action.

Daivam vinātiprayatanam karoti yattadwiphalam = A work done well under a plan yields good results even though the fate is in opposition.

Asamāhitasya vritirna vidyate = A restless mind knows no etiquette.

Purvam nishchatya pashchāt kāryamārbhet = After a good deal of deliberation and determination, one should start a work.

Kāryāntare deerghasutrita nā kartavyā = Do not delay a work after starting it.

Nā chalchitasya kāryāwāptih = A restless person fails to finish a work.

Hastgatāwamānanāt kāryavyatikramo bhawati = One should utilise everything available in order to finish a work.

Doshavarjitāni kāryāni durlabhāni = It is difficult to get a man free of weaknesses and a work free of mistakes.

Duranubandham kāryam nārambhet = One should not start a work which cannot be finished.

Kālavit kāryam sādhayet = The man who knows the right time succeeds in his work.

Kālātikramāt kāla yeva phalam pibati = The time itself destroys the work when the time of work is over.

Kshanam prati kālavikshepam nā kuryāt sarvakrityeshu = One should never delay in a fixed duty.

Deshaphalabibhagau gyātwā kāryamarbhet = One should start a work after carefully considering time, place and situation.

Daivahinam kāryam susādhyamapi duhsādhyam bhawati = When the fate opposes, an easy task becomes unachievable.

Nitigyo deshkālau parikshet = To make conscious effort is the first duty of a wise man.

Parikshyakārini shrishwaram tishthati = He gets success who does a work after carefully examining everything.

Sarvāshcha sampadah sarvopāyena parigrahet = A king should acquire wealth with every means at his control.

Bhāgyawantamparikshyakārinim shrih parityajati = Goddess Lakshmi abandons them who start a work without examining the opportunities.

Gyānenānumānaishcha parikshā kartavyā = One should use his mental agility, experiences and the power to think to know how a work can be accomplished.

Yo yasmin karmani kushalah tam tasminyeva yojayeta = One should be asked to perform such duties in which he is an expert.

Duhsādhyamapi susādhyam karoti upāyagyah = By adopting and employing proper ways and means, a difficult task can be accomplished easily.

Agyāninākritamapi nā bahu mantavyam = One should not attach great importance to a work accomplished by an ignorant man.

Yādrichchikatwāt krimirapi rupāntarāni karoti = When a wood-worm changes the face of a plank, it cannot be taken as great art.

Siddhasyaiva kāryasya prakāshanam kartavyam = One should declare only that which has already been achieved.

Gyānawatāmapi daivamānushadoshāt kāryāni dushyanti = Many works remain unfinished because of fate, situation or a silly mistake by someone.

Daivam shāntikarmanā pratishedhavyam = At the time of natural calamity, one should remain calm and cool and try to get out of that calamity.

Mānushim kāryavipattim kaushalena viniwārayet = The problems created by human beings should be wisely tackled.

Kāryavipatau doshān varnayanti bālishāh = After failure, fools repent or try to pass the buck on others.

Kāryārthinā dākshinyam nā kartavyam = The officers who wish to get success should never have compassion and sympathy towards the enemies.

Ksheerārthi vatso mātrirudhah pratihanti = The calf attacks the udder of his own mother for sucking milk.

Aprayatnāt kāryavipattirbhawati = Without adequate effort, a work is destroyed.

Nā daivapramānānam kāryasiddhih = They fail to complete a task who start with a doubt.

Kāryabāhyo nā poshayatyāshritān = They fail to foster their dependents who do not perform their duties.

Yah kāryam nā pashyati soandhah = He is blind who does not realise his duties.

Pratyakshaparokshānumānaih kāryāni parikshet = One should consider well the available and non-available materials before starting a work.

Aparikshyakārinam shrih parityajati = Goddess Lakshmi abandons him and he becomes unsuccessful who starts a work without taking into consideration all its aspects.

Parikshya tāryā vipattih = One should wisely tackle the problems that come while at work.

Swashaktim gyātwā kāryamārbhet = One should weigh one's capacity before starting a work.

Swajanam tarpayitwā yah sheshabhoji soamritabhoji = He consumes nectar as food who feeds his relatives and dependents before taking his own meal.

Sarvānushthānadāyamukhāni vardhante = The country where many types of work are usually in progress gets rich.

Nāsti bheeroh kāryachintā = Cowards are not worried about their works.

Swāminah sheelam gyātwā kāryārthi kāryam sādhayati = The dependents perform their duties according to the need and mood of their masters.

Dhenoh sheelagyah ksheeram bhunkte = By knowing the nature of a cow, a person can be able to milk her.

Kshudre guhyaprakāshanam ātmawānna kuryāt = A wise man should not volunteer secret to his freakish and low-bred servant.

Āshritairpyawamanyate mriduswabhāwah = A humble man is humiliated by his dependents.

Teekshnadandah sarvairudwejaniyo bhawati = Unproportionately high punishment for a minor crime makes a ruler a figure of hatred.

Yathārhadandakāri syāt = It is better for a king to announce right punishment.

Alpasāram shrutawantamapi nā bahu manyate lokah = A learned man is not accepted as learned, if he is not serious.

Atibhārah purushamawasādayati = The man with excessive load gets tired too soon and forsakes the work.

Yah sansadi pardosham shansati sa swadoshabahutwam prakhyāpyati = In an assembly or a parliament that man declares himself to be full of faults (a criminal) who starts criticising something or someone out of prejudice.

Ātmānamyeva nāshayati anātmawatām kopah = The unrefined fellows bring harm to themselves by meaningless anger.

Nāstyaprāpyam satyawatām = Those who possess the wealth of truth possess everything.

Sāhasena nā kāryasiddhirbhawati = One cannot succeed only on courage.

Vyasanārto vismaratyapraveshena = An addicted person fails to concentrate and forgets his duties.

Nāstyanantarāyah kālbikshepe = He who wastes his time cannot lead an easy life.

Asansayavimāshāt sansayavināshah shreyān = One cannot avoid the ultimate end by avoiding struggle. It is better to die an uncertain death while engrossed in struggle than to wait for the definite death.

Upardhanāni niksheptuh kewalam swārtham = He who cannot protect the trust and money of others will always think of his own lustful gain.

Dānam dharmah = Charity is duty (religion).

Tadwiparito anarthasevi = He destroys the peace who thinks against religion and prosperity.

Rijuswabhāwo janeshu durlabhah = The people of balanced nature are rare.

Awamānenāgatmaiswryamwamanyate sādhuh = A gentleman will not accept money which is earned by evil means.

Bahunapi gunāneko dosho grasate = One evil destroys many virtues.

Mahātmanā parena sāhasam nā kartavyam = Sublime persons should not depend on others for important works.

Kadāchidapi charitram nā langhayet = One should not forsake human values even under difficult circumstances.

Kshudhārtho nā trinam charati singhah = Though hungry, yet a lion will not eat grass.

Prānādapi pratayayo rakshitavyah = One should keep faith even at the cost of one's life.

Pishunah shrotā putradārārapi tyajayate = A faithless person is deserted by his own son and wife.

Satyamapyashradheyam nā vadet = Do not say anything about truth to a person who has no faith in truth.

Nālpadoshād bahugunāstyajyante = One's great qualities cannot be rejected because of his minor bad habits.

Bipaschitswapi sulabhā doshāh = Bad qualities can be detected in any great person.

Nāstiratnamakhanditam = There is no jewel without some deformity.

Maryādāteetam nā kadāchidapi viswaset = Do not keep faith in such men who break the social and moral codes.

Apriye kritam priyamapi dweshyam bhawati = Be alert when an enemy behaves well.

Nā mantyapi tulākotih kupodakachhayam karoti = Like the bucket that enters the water of a well humbly and comes out with water, one should be beware of the enemy who pretends to be humble.

Satām matam nātikramet = One should never disprove the decisions taken by sublime persons.

Mritpindoapi pātaligandhamutpādayati = As the soil takes fragrance from the flowers, in the same way one can take virtue from sublime souls.

Rajatam kanaksangāt kanakam bhawati = In the company of gold, silver too becomes gold.

Upakartaryapakartumichchhatyabadhuh = A foolish and cruel person deceives his own helper for lustful gain.

Nā pāpakarmanākroshabhayam = Wicked sinners are not afraid of and do not feel ashamed even when condemned.

Utasāhwatām shatrawoapi bashibhawanti = Over-enthusiastic persons can win over their terrific enemies.

Vikramadhanā rājānah = Valour is the greatest wealth of a king.

Nāstyalsasyaihikāmusmikam = Laziness destroys a person.

Nirutsāhādaivam patati = Lack of enthusiasm guarantees failure.

Matasyārthiva jalamupayutyārtham grihiniyāt = As one who wishes to catch fish must enter water, in the same manner one must try for something to achieve.

Aviswasteshu viswāso nā kartavyah = Do not believe the persons who have not been tested as yet.

Bisham bishamyeva sarvakālam = Poison will always remain poison.

Arthasamādāne vairinām sang yeva nā kartavyah = For accomplishing something, one should not take help from enemies.

Arthasidhau vairinam nā viswaset = For accomplishing something, one should not keep faith on the enemies.

Arthādheena yeva niyatasambandhah = The relations are formed and kept for one's own purpose and gain.

Shatrorapisutasshakhā rakshitavyah = One must save a friend even if he is the son of an enemy.

Yāwadchhatroshchhidram pashyati tāwaddhastena wā skandhena wā wāhyah = One must feign friendship with the enemy whom one wishes to attack and destroy.

Shatru chhidre pariharet = Know the weakness of the enemy and exploit it.

Ātmachchidram nā prakāshayet = Do not show your own weakness.

Chhidraprahārinashshatrawah = Strike your enemy at his weak spots.

Hastagatamapi shatrum nā viswaset = A king should not believe the captured king.

Swajanasya durvritam niwārayet = One should try to free the near and dear ones from vices and weaknesses.

Swajanāwamānoapi manaswinām dukhamvwahati = It brings disgrace when the men of one's side are wicked. It is painful.

Ekāngadoshah purushamawasādayati = The pain of one wound is felt by the whole body, in the same way the dubious nature of one man blackens the fame of a society or kingdom or government.

Shatrum jayati subrittatā = An enemy can be won over only by sublimity in character.

Nikritipriyā neechāh = The wicked deceive the gentle folks.

Neechasya matirna dātavyā = The wicked should not be given moral lessons.

Teshu viswāso nā kartavyah = A wicked person should never be believed.

Supujitoapi durjanah peedayatyyeva = A wicked person will deceive even when treated well.

Chandanādeenapi dāwāgnirdahatyyeva = The fire of the forest destroys even the sandalwood trees despite their virtues and fragrance.

Kadāpi purusham nāwamanyet = One should not show disrespect to any man.

Kshantavyamiti purusham nā bādhet = Forgiveness is human nature. One should not bring harm to anyone.

Bhartrādhikam rahasyayuktam vaktumichhantya buddhayah = Fools open the resolutions taken secretly by a king before them.

Anurāstu phalena suchyate = The result proclaims the love.

Agyāphalamaishwaryam = Prosperity is the outcome of wisdom.

Dātavyamapibālishah kleshena paridāsyati = A fool feels aggrieved while giving a thing to its rightful owner.

Mahadaishwaryam prāpyāpyadhritimān vinashayati = Fools perish despite inheriting great wealth.

Nāstyadhriteraihikāmushmikam = A restless person gets neither physical nor spiritual pleasure.

Nā durjanaih sah sansargah kartavyah = Do not keep the company of the wicked.

Shoundahastagatam payo apyawamanyate = Milk will also be taken as wine in the hand of a wine-dealer.

Kārya sankateshwartha vyawasāyini budhih = That is practical wisdom which solves the problems that arise while completing a work.

Mitabhojanam swāstham = He remains healthy who eats a bit less than needed.

Pathyamapyapathyājeerne nāshniyāt = At the time of disorder in digestive system, one should not take even easily digestible food.

Jeernabhojinam vyādhirnopasarpati = He remains healthy who eats only after the earlier food is digested.

Jeernashareere vardhamānam vyādhirnopekshayet = During weakness in body (mostly during old age), one should not ignore diseases.

Ajeerne bhojanam dukham = When suffering from indigestion, food is painful.

Shatrorapi vishishyate vyādhih = Diseases are greater and more powerful than enemies.

Dānam nidhānamanugāmi = One should spend in charity only according to one's capability.

Patutare trishnāpare sulabhamatisandhānam = One should be alert against the persons who suddenly try to grow intimacy.

Trishnayā matishchhādyate = Lust puts a veil on the conscience.

Kāryabahutwe bahuphalamāyatikam kuryāt = When there are many options, one should select the work which has some permanent value.

Swayamevāwaskannam kāryam nirikshet = One should correct one's mistakes made while expediting a work.

Murkheshu sāhasam niyatam = To be adventurous is the nature of fools.

Murkheshu vivdam nā kartavyah = One should not start a debate with the fools.

Murkheshu murkhawat kathayet = One should behave like a fool with a fool.

Āyasairāyasam chhedyam = Iron cuts iron.

Nāstyadhamitah sakhā = Fools have no real friends.

Dharmena dhāryate lokah = The world can be kept intact only by religion.

Pretamapi dharmādhrmāwanugachhatah = The wholesome and unwholesome deeds of a person accompany him after his death.

Dayā dharmasya janmabhumih = Pity is the birthplace of religion.

Dharmamule satyadāne = Religion is the basis of truth and charity.

Dharmena jayati lokān = Religion makes one win the world.

Mrityurapi dharmishtham rakshati = A religious person does not perish even after death.

Dharmādwiparitam pāpam yatra prasajyate tatra dharmāwamatirmahati prasajyeta = When vices become stronger, they bring disgrace to the religion.

Upasthitavināshānām prakrityākārena lakshyate = Stronger opposition of religion by the sinners or demons foretells their annihilation.

Pishunavādino rahasyam = One should not open a secret to backbiters and falsehood mongers.

Pararahasyam naiva shrotavyam = One should not listen to the secrets of others.

Ballabhasya kārakatwadharmayuktam = Cruelty of the master is not treated in good humour.

Swajaneshwatikramo nā kartavyah = One should not ignore one's near and dear ones.

Mātāpi dushtā tyājyā = A wicked mother too should be forsaken.

Swahastoapi bishdigdhashchhedyah = One should cut off one's own hand if it has become poisonous.

Paroapi cha hito bandhu = Without being actually related if one extends helping hands, he should be treated as a friend.

Kakshādapyoushadham grihyate = One can take medicines even from dried up forests.

Nāsti choureshu viswāsah = Thieves cannot be believed.

Apratikāreshwanāderah nā kartavyah = If the work is going on smoothly, one should not take it for granted and ignore it.

Vyasanam manāgapi bādhate = Calamity or addiction should not be ignored as insignificant.

Amarwadarthajātamarjayet = One should keep on collecting useful things as if he is immortal.

Arthawān sarvalokasya bahumatah = Rich people get honour everywhere.

Mahendrumapyarthaheenam nā bahu manyate lokah = A poor king does not get honour.

Dāridryam khalu purushashya jeevitam maranam = A poor person is treated as dead even when alive.

Birupo arthawān surupah = A rich man is treated as handsome though he might be ugly.

Adātāram apyarthawantam arthino nā tyajanti = Those who wish to accumulate wealth expect money even from the misers.

Akulino api kulinādwishishthah = A low-born rich man is better than a high-born, if he spends his wealth in social causes.

Nāstya mānabhayam anāryasya = A man without standing is not afraid of insult and contempt.

Nā chetanwatām vritibhayam = A skilled person is not afraid of unemployment.

Nā jeetendiyānām vishaya bhayam = A man who has control over his sense organs is not afraid of lust.

Nā kritārthānām marana bhayam = He who has done a lot of good things is not afraid of death.

Kasyachidartham swamiwa manyate sādhuh = Sublime persons treat the wealth of other persons as trust-property.

Parbibhaweswādaro nā kartavyah = One should not have lust for others' wealth.

Parbibhaweswādaropi bināshamulam = The lust for others' wealth becomes the cause of ruin.

Palālamapi paradravyam nā hartavyam = One should not steal wealth of other persons even equal to a straw.

Pardravya upaharanam ātmadravya nāshahetuh = Stealing becomes the cause of the destruction of one's own wealth.

Nā chourāt param mrityu pāshah = There is no trap deadlier than stealing.

Yawāgurapi prāna dhāranam karoti loke = The pulse of oat is enough to keep one alive if it is available at the right time.

Nā mritasya aushadham prayojanam bhawati = No medicine is required after death.

Samkāle swayamapi prabhutwasya prayojanam bhawati = During peaceful days, only to sustain becomes a duty.

Neechasya vidyā pāpakarmani yojayanti = The knowledge and skill of a wicked person draws him towards vices.

Payah pānamapi bishavardhanam bhujangasya nāmritam syāt = Giving milk to a snake adds to its poison, the milk does not change it into nectar.

Nahi dhānyasamo hyarthah = There is nothing more useful for life than grain.

Nā kshudhā samah shatruh = There is no enemy greater than hunger.

Akriterniyatā kshut = Lazy and workless usually go without food.

Indriyāni jarābasham kurwanti = Misuse of the sense organs brings the old age untimely.

Sānukrosham bhartāram ājeewet = One should serve a kind and gentle master.

Lubdhasevi pāwakechchhayā khadyotam dhamati = The result of serving a miser master is similar to that who tries to obtain fire from a firefly by fanning it.

Visheshagyam swāminamāshrayet = One should try to obtain a learned or specialist master.

Purushasya maithunam jarā = Sex makes a man old.

Strinām amaithunam jarā = A lady grows old without sex.

Nā neechottamayorvivāhah = A relation by marriage should not be established between high and low.

Agamyāgamanādāyuryashah punyāni ksheeyante = One loses age, prestige and virtue by visiting a prostitute.

Nāstyahankāasamah shatru = There is no enemy like ego and pride.

Sansadi shatrum nā parikroshet = One should not abuse an enemy in an assembly.

Shatru vyasanam shravan shukham = The news of bad habits or of the downfall of an enemy gives pleasure.

Adhansya buddhih nā bidyate = A poor man loses his mental agility.

Hitamapyadhanasya vākyam nā shrinoti = A poor man's good advices are also ignored.

Adhanah swabhāryayā apyawamanyate = Even the wife of a poor man shows disrespect towards him.

Pushpaheenam sahkāramapi nopāsate bhramarāh = As a flowerless mango tree is forsaken by black bees, in the same way a poor man is left alone.

Vidyā dhanam adhanānām = Knowledge is the wealth of the poor.

Vidyā chourairapi nā grāhyā = Knowledge cannot be stolen.

Vidyayā khyāpitā khyātih = With knowledge one gets fame.

Yashah shariram nā vinashayati = The abstract body of fame is never destroyed.

Yah parārtham upasarpati sa satpurushah = He who helps others is a sublime person.

Indriyānām prasham shastram = Sense organs can be controlled by reading treatises and scriptures.

Ashastra kāryabritau shāshtrānkusham niwārayati = Only treatises and scriptures can control a person who is ready to commit a crime.

Neechasya vidyā nopetavyā = The knowledge of the wicked should be ignored.

Malechchha bhāshanam nā shikshet = One should not use filthy language.

Malechchānāmapi subritam grāhyam = Good ideas should be taken even from demonic persons.

Gune nā matsarah kartavyah = One should not be jealous of others' great qualities.

Shatrorapi suguno grāhya = One should take good qualities even from enemies.

Bishādapyamritam grāhyam = The nectar from the poison can be taken.

Awasthayā purushah sammānyate = Man becomes honourable under certain difficult circumstances.

Sthān yyeva narāh pujyante = People get honour at their respective places.

Āryavrittam anutishthet = A man should follow the refined (Aryan) people.

Kadāpi maryādām nā atikramet = Never break the moral barriers.

Nāstyarghah purushratnasya = Learned and highly skilled persons are jewels.

Nā striratna samam ratnam = There is no jewel better than a woman.

Sudurlabham ratnam = It is very difficult to get jewels.

Ayasho bhayam bhayeshu = The fear of notoriety is the greatest fear.

Nāstya alsasya shāshtādhigam = A lazy person cannot understand the classics and the scriptures.

Nā stranasya swargāptih dharmakrityam cha = A man engrossed in women (or an effeminate) can neither perform religious activities nor get heaven.

Strioapi stranamwamanyate = Even women insult an effeminate.

Nā pushpārthi sinchati shushkatarum = One who wants flowers will not irrigate a dry tree.

Adravya prayatno bālukāquathanādananyah = To work for nothing and to try to squeeze out oil from sand are the same things.

Nā mahājanhāsah kartavyah = Do not laugh at great men.

Kārya sampadam nimittāni suchayanti = The very appearance of a work signifies whether it is profitable or not.

Nakshadrāpi nimittāni visheshayanti = Special meanings are derived from the constellation of stars.

Nā twaritasya nakshatra parikshā = A diligent person does not examine his efforts with reference to the constellation of stars.

Parichaye doshā nā chhadyante = The weaknesses come out after introduction.

Swayam shudhah parānāshankate = An impure person doubts the integrity of others.

Swabhāwo duratikramah = It is difficult to change the nature.

Uparādha anurupo dandah = Punishment should be in accordance with the crime.

Kathānurupam prativachanam = The answer must be proper, congruent to the question.

Bibhāwānurupam ābharanam = One should wear ornaments according to one's financial capacity.

Kulānurupam vrittam = One should work in accordance with one's family tradition.

Kāryānurupam prayatanam = One should make efforts according to the need of the work.

Pātānurupam dānam = Gift should be given congruent to the personality.

Vayonurupo veshah = Dress should be in accordance with age.

Swāmyanukulo bhritya = A servant should be harmonical to the master.

Bhartribashavartani bhāryā = A wife should be under the control of her husband.

Gurubashānuvartani shishyah = A disciple should be under the control of the teacher.

Pitrivashānuvartani putah = A son should be obedient to his father.

Atyupchārah shankitavyah = Extra care (and honour) raises doubts.

Swāmini kupite swāminamewānubartet = A servant should work in conformity with the master's mood when he is angry.

Mātri tādito vatso mātaramewānurodati = A child beaten by mother weeps to her.

Snehawatah swalpo hi roshah = The anger of one who loves does not last.

Ātma chhidram nā pashyati parchchhidramyeva pashyat bālishah = A fool is not conscious of his own faults; he finds faults with others.

Sopachārah kaitawah = A cunning person shows great service.

Kāmyaih visheshairupacharanam upachārah = Something done with special intention is known as service.

Chiraparichita anām atyupachārah shankitavyah = Excessive service by known persons raises doubt.

Gaurduskarā shwasahashrād ekākini shreyasi = One cow is far better than a hundred dogs.

Shwo mayurād adya kapoto varah = Today's pigeon is better than tomorrow's peacock.

Atiprasango dosham utpādyati = Excessive indulgence (extra enthusiasm) degenerates.

Sarvam jayatya akrodhah = A man without anger makes friends and wins them.

Yadyapakārini kopah kope kopa yyeva kartavyah = If one has to show anger, then before showing it on sinners, one must show anger against one's anger.

Matimatsu murkha-mitra-guru-ballabheshu vivādo nā kartavyah = Do not engage in discussion or debate against fools, friends, teachers and masters.

Nāstya pishācham aishwaryam = Demonic spirit is an integral part of wealth and prosperity.

Nāsti dhanwatām sukarmasu shramah = The rich can easily perform good deeds.

Nāsti gatishramo yānaawatām = He does get tired who travels on a vehicle.

Alohamayam nigadam kalatram = Women are chains without iron.

Yo yasmin kushalah sa tasmin yoktavyah = One should be engaged in the work one is expert in.

Duskalatram manaswinām sharira karshanam = A wicked wife weakens a learned man.

Apramato dārān nirikshet = Without being lazy, one should be vigilant over one's wife.

Strishu kinchid api nā viswaset = One should not believe a woman.

Nā samādhih strishu lokagyatā cha = Women lack concentration and social consciousness.

Gurunām mātā gariyasi = A mother is greater among the teachers.

Sarva awasthāsu mātā bhartavyā = Under all circumstances, a mother should be fed.

Vaidushyam alankārena āchchhadyate = Artificiality draws a veil over scholarship.

Strinām bhushanam lajjā = Shyness is a woman's ornament.

Viprānām bhushanam Vedam = Knowledge is a Brahmin's ornament.

Sarvoshām bhushanam dharmah = Religion is everyone's ornament.

Bhushanānām bhushanam savinayā vidya = The ornament of all ornaments is knowledge with humility.

Anupadravam deshamāwaset = Live in a country where there is no terror.

Sādhujanabahulo deshah = A true country is the one which is dominated by gentle citizens.

Rāgyo bhetavyam sarvakālakam = One should always be afraid of the ruler.

Nā rāgyah param daivatam = There is no god greater than a king.

Suduram api dahati rājawanhi = A king's fire burns afar.

Riktahasto nā rājānam abhigachchet = One should not go to a king empty-handed.

Gurum cha daivam cha = One should not go empty-handed to a guru and God.

Kutumbino bhetavyam = One should fear the relatives of a king.

Gantavyam sadā rājakulam = One should keep on visiting the court of a king.

Rājapurushaih sambandham kuryāt = One should maintain good relations with government officials.

Rājadāsi nā sevitavyā = One should not develop any relation with a king's maid.

Nā chakshushāpi rājadhanam nirikshet = One should not have lust for king's property.

Putre gunawati kutumbinah swargah = A son with sublime qualities is like heaven for the relatives.

Putrā vidyānām pāram gamiyatām = One should make his sons experts in every discipline.

Jana padārtham grāmam tyajet = For the benefit of general mass, the interests of a village can be sacrificed.

Grāmārtham kutumbasya tyajet = For the benefit of the village, the interests of the relatives can be sacrificed.

Atilābhah putralābhah = The best gain is the birth of a son.

Prāyena hi putrāh pitaramanuvartante = Usually sons follow the path of their fathers.

Durgateh pitarau rakshati saputrah = He is the real son who saves his parents during adversity.

Kulam prakhyāpayati putrah = A son brings fame to a family.

Yen tat kulam prakhyātam sah purushah = He is a man who gives name and fame to the family tradition.

Nā anapatyasya swargah = There is no heaven without a son.

Yā prasute sā bhāryā = She who gives birth to a child is a wife.

Sateerthā abhigamanād brahcharyam nashyati = A close relationship between a girl and a boy studying under the same guru (institution) destroys bachelorship and virginity.

Putrārthā hi striyah = Women are accepted only for sons.

Swadāsiparigraho hi swadāsa bhāwah = To marry (to develop relation with) a maid is to become a servant.

Upasthita bināshah pathyavākyam nā shrinoti = When destruction is close, one does not listen to saviour advice.

Nāsti dehinām sukhadukha abhāwah = There is no dearth of pleasure and pain for the body.

Mātermiwa vatsāh sukhdukhāni kartārmewa anugachchhanti = As a calf goes to its mother, in the same way pleasure and pain reach their respective destinations.

Tilamātramapya upakāram shailmātram manyte sādhuh = An insignificant assistance is taken as a mountain of help by sublime figures.

Upakāro anāryeshwa kartavyah = One should not help the wicked.

Pratyupakāra bhayād anāryah shatrurbhawati = Out of the fear that he might may be required to reciprocate the help, a wicked man turns enemy.

Swalpamapy upakārkrite pratyupakāram kartum aryo nā swapiti = Men with sublime nature are ready to do a lot for a little.

Nā kadāpi dyevatā awamantakā = One should not insult the gods.

Nā chakshushah samam jyotirasti = There is no light equal to eyes.

Chakshurhi shareerinām netā = Eyes are the leader of the body.

Upachakshushah kim shareerena = There is no meaning of a body without eyes.

Nā apsu mutram kuryāt = Do not pass urine under water.

Nā nagno jalam pravishet = Do not enter water when naked.

Yathā shareeram tathā gyānam = The appearance shows the knowledge.

Yathā buddhistathā bibhawah = One earns proportionate to one's wisdom.

Agnāwagnim nā nikshipet = Do not put fire into fire.

Tapaswinah pujaneeyāh = One who observes austerity should be worshipped.

Pardārān nā gachchhet = One should not have immoral relation with someone else's wife.

Annadānam bhruna hatyāmapi pramārshti = One can be free from the crime of destroying an embryo by giving grain in charity.

Nā Veda bāhyo dharmah = There is no religion away from the Vedas.

Nā kadāchidapi dharmam nishedhayet = Religion should never be opposed.

Swargam nayati sunritam = Sweet tongue helps in reaching heaven.

Nāsti satyātparam tapah = There is no penance greater than truth.

Satyam swargasya sādhanam = Truth is a staircase to heaven.

Satyena dharyate lokah = Truth is the foundation of the world.

Satyād devo barshati = Truth is blessed by gods.

Nānritāt pātakam param = There is no greater sin than falsehood.

Nā mimāmsā guruwah = One should not criticise a teacher.

Khalatwam nopeyāt = Wickedness should never be accepted.

Nāsti khalasya mitram = The wicked have no friends.

Lokayātrā daridram bādhate = Life is difficult for the poor.

Atishuro dānashurah = A charitable person is the strongest warrior.

Gurudyevabrahamneshu bhaktir bhushanam = Devotion towards the teacher, God and Brahmin is an ornament.

Sarbasya bhushanam binayah = Humility is everyone's ornament.

Akulino api vinitah kulinādwishishtah = A low-born humble person is better than an arrogant high-born.

Āchārād āyurvardhate kirtishcha = Lifespan and fame increase by proper and gentle behaviour.

Priyamapyahitam nā vaktavyam = Though beneficial, yet do not speak unpleasant truth.

Bahujana biruddham ekam nā anuvartet = Do not follow the one who is being opposed by many.

Nā durjaneshu bhāgafheyah kartavyah = One should not attach one's future with a wicked person.

Nā kritārtheshu neecheshu sambandhah = Though successful in his business, yet one should not keep relation with the wicked.

Rinashatruvyādhishwasheshah kartavyah = One should finish debt, enemy and disease.

Bhutyanuvartanam purushashya rasāyanam = To proceed on the path of welfare is the best chemical for men.

Nārthiswa awagyā kāryā = Do not insult a beggar.

Sudushkaram karmam kāryitwā kartāram awamanyate neechah = With a view to insult a person, a wicked man gets a difficult work done by a gentleman.

Nākritagyasya narakānniwartanam = Ungrateful have no place to go but the hell.

Jihwā yattau vriddhivinshau = Both progress and annihilation are on the tongue of a man.

Bishamritayoh ākaro jihwā = Both nectar and poison are on the tongue of a man.

Priyavādino nā shatruh = A soft-spoken man has no enemy.

Stutā api dyevatā stusyanti = With prayer, even gods are pleased.

Anritam api durvachanam chiram tishthati = A false allegation remains afresh in memory for a long time.

Rājadwishtam nā cha vaktavyam = One should not say anything which can start enmity with the king.

Shrutisukhāt kokilālāpātushyanti = Though black in appearance, a cuckoo bird is liked by all because of its sheet voice.

Swadharmahetuh satpurushah = For following their own religion, humble persons are liked and called gentle.

Nāstyarthino gauravam = A beggar gets no respect.

Strnām bhushanam saubhāgyam = Husband is the ornament of a woman.

Shatro api nā pataneeyā vriti = The cause of livelihood of even an enemy should not be obliterated.

Aprayatnādekam kshetram = The cultivable land is the one where water is available without much effort.

Arandam awalambya kunjaram nā kopayet = An elephant should not show anger if it has taken the shelter of a castor-oil plant.

Atiprabriddhā shālmali wārana stambho nā bhawati = Though very old and strong, yet an elephant cannot be tied to silk-cotton tree.

Ati deergho karnikaro nā musali = Even a very big oleander stem cannot be a pestle.

Atideepto api khadyoto nā pāwakah = Though very bright, yet a firefly cannot give fire.

Nā prabhudhatwam gunahetuh = A rich cannot necessarily be qualified.

Sujeernoh api pichumando nā shangkulāyate = Despite being old, a neem tree cannot be a nut-cracker.

Yathā beejam tathā nispati = A plant depends on the seed.

Yathā shrutam tathā buddhih = The mind is influenced by what one listens to.

Yathā kulam tathā āchāram = The behaviour of a man depends on his family tradition.

Samskritah pichumando nā sahkāro bhawati = Howsoever the neem is purified, it cannot turn into a mango.

Swayamyeva dukham adhigachchhati = Suffering depends on the deeds.

Nā rātri chāranamk kuryāt = Do not move during the night.

Nā cha ardharatram swapeyāt = Do not keep awake after midnight.

Tadwidwadwibhih pariksheta = One should learn from the elders and learned men what is to be done and when it should be done.

Pargrihamakāranato nā pravishet = One should not enter another man's house.

Gyātwā api doshamyeva karoti lokah = Man becomes a criminal knowingly.

Shastrapradhānā lokavritih = We should behave as written in the classics and scriptures.

Shāshtrābhāve shishtāchāram anugachchhet = In the absence of classics and scriptures (the knowledge of such books), one should follow the elders.

Nācharitāchchhāstram gariyah = The classics are not better than the character.

Durastham api chārchakshuh pashyati rājāh = Despite being away, a king is able to look with his four eyes.

Gatānugatiko lokah = The mass follows the tradition.

Yamanujeevettam nāpawadet = That which provides livelihood should not be abused.

Tapahsrah indriyanigrah = The essence of penance is to control the senses.

Durlabhah stribandhanānmokshah = It is difficult to get free from the grip of woman.

Strinām sarva ashubhānām kshetram = Women are the field of all bad omens.

Ashubhadweshinah strishu nā prasaktāh = Those who do not want to get ruined do not fall for women.

Yagyaphalagyāh trivedavidah = He who knows the *Tri-Vedas* knows the result of a research.

Swargasthānam nā shāshwatam = Heaven is not a permanent gain.

Yāwatpunyaphalam tāwadyeva swargaphalam = One can remain in heaven till one has the power of one's virtues and good deeds.

Nā cha swarga patanāt param dukham = There is no fall more painful than to fall from the heaven.

Dehi deham tyaktwā aindrapadam nā wanchhati = Man does not want to get the position of the Lord of Heaven in lieu of his body.

Dukhānām aushadham nirvānam = Liberation is the medicine of suffering.

Anarya sambandha aduttam ārya shatrutā = To be an enemy of a humble man is far better than to be a friend of a wicked man.

Nihanti durvachanam kulam = Abusive language destroys the fame of a family tradition.

Nā puta sansaparshāt param sukham = There is no pleasure greater than touching a son.

Vivāde dharmam anusaret = When there is doubt and debate, follow the religion.

Nishānte kāryam chintayeta = One should plan the days work at the end of the night (during the early hours of the morning).

Upasthita bināsho durnayam manyate = When annihilation comes closer, one indulges into immoral acts.

Ksheerārthinah kim karinyā = One who wishes to get milk would not buy an elephant.

Nā dānasamam vashyam = There is no magical enchantment than charity.

Parāyatteshu utkanthā nā kuryāt = Do not wish to get things in others' possession.

Asadasya samridhih asadamyeva bhujyate = The wicked enjoy the property of the wicked.

Nimbphalam kākaih bhujyate = The bitter fruit of neem is eaten only by the crows.

Nā ambhodadhih trishnām apohati = The salty water of the sea does not quench the thirst.

Bālukā api swagunam āshrayante = Sand will not forsake its qualities.

Santoasatsu nā ramante = The gentle do not feel comfortable among the wicked.

Nā hansā pretavane ramante = A swan does not like to live in the graveyards.

Athārtham parvatate lokah = All of us run after money.

Āshayā badhyate lokah = We sustain with hope.

Nā cha āshāparaih shrih sah tishthati = Only hope will not obtain money (Goddess Lakshmi).

Āshāpare nā dhairyam = A man with only hope has little patience.

Dainyān maranam uttamam = It is better to die than to live in penury condition.

Āshā lajjām vyapohati = Hope makes one shameless.

Ātmā nā stotavya = One should not praise oneself.

Nā divā swapanam kuryāt = One should not dream or sleep during the day.

Āyuh kshayee divā nidrā = One loses longevity by sleeping during the day.

Nā chāsannam api pashyatyaishwaryāndhah nā shrinotishtam = A man blinded by his wealth neither sees nor listens to anything.

Strinām nā bharth param daivatam = There is no greater God than husband for a woman.

Tadanuvartanam ubhayasoukhyam = The woman who follows her husband gets both the worldly and heavenly pleasures.

Atithim abhyāgatam pujayed yathābidhih = A guest should be welcomed courteously.

Nityam sambibhāgi syāt = One must share his daily earning too.

Nāsti habyasya byāghāt = The best offered to the deserving is not a waste.

Shatruh api pramādi lobhāt = Lust will deviate the enemy.

Shatruh mitrawat pratibhāti = An enemy appears to be a friend.

Mrigatrishnā jalwad bhāti = Because of thirst, a deer takes sand to be water.

Upālambho nāstya pranayeshu = There is no gain in complaining to an arrogant.

Durmedha sāmaschchhāstram mohayati = The commonplace publications make a fool out of an ill-read person.

Satsangah swargvāshah = To be in saintly congregation is to live in heaven.

Āryah swameo param manyate = Sublime persons take others to be sublime.

Rupānuvarti gunah = The qualities must be in accordance with the appearance.

Yatra sukham vartate tadyeva sthānam = That is the best place where one can live happily and peacefully.

Vishwāsghātino nā nishkritih = There is no respite or expiation for a treacherous person.

Daivāyattam nā shochet = One should not worry about that which is not under our control.

Āshrtadukham ātman yeva manyate sādhuh = Gentle persons take the pain of their dependents as their own.

Hridgatamāchchhādyānyadwadatyanāyah = He is a wicked person who hides the reality to misguide others.

Buddhiheenah pishāchād ananyah = A fool is like a goblin.

Asahāyah pathi nā gachhet = One should not travel alone.

Putro nā stotabyah = Do not praise your son.

Swāmi satotabyo anujivibhih = Servants should keep on praising their master.

Dharmakrteswapi swāmina yeva ghoshayet = A government official should declare his own deeds done for general good as the work of the ruler.

Rājāgyā nātilanghayet = One should not disobey a king.

Swāmyanugrahi dharmakrityam bhrityānām = To get praise from the master for good performance is the duty of the servants.

Yathā agyaptam tathā kuryet = One should do as one is ordered.

Savisesham wā kuryāt = Something special and profitable can be done without permission.

Swāmino bheeruh kwopayujyte = Fearful persons have no place in a government.

Nāstya anāryasya kripa = One cannot expect a helping hand from a wicked person.

Nāsti buddhimatām shatruh = A wise man has no enemy.

Shatrm nā nindayet sabhāyām = One should not deplore an enemy in a meeting.

Shaktau kshamā shalāghaniyā = The strong are praised for forgiveness.

Kshamāwān yeva sarvam sādhayati = One who forgives succeeds at every place.

Āpadartham dhanam rakshet = One should save money for emergency.

Sāhasamwatām priyam kartavyam = The courageous love their duty.

Swah kāryamadya kurvit = Do the work of tomorrow today.

Aparāhinakam purvāhnā yevam kartavyam = The work of evening should be completed before noon.

Vyawahārānulomo dharmah = Religion should be practical.

Sarvgyatā lokgyatā = To know the society is to know all.

Shastragyo apyalokagyo murkhotulyah = Though well-read, yet if one fails to know the society, then he is like a fool.

Shāshta prayojanam tatwadarshanam = The aim of the classics is to know the essence.

Tatwagyānam kāryameva prakāshayati = The knowledge of the essence comes by practical work.

Vyawahāre pakshapāto nā kāryah = One should not give extra advantage in common practice.

Dharmādapi vyawahāro gariyān = Practice is more difficult than the theory of religion.

Ātmā hi vyawahārasya sākshi = The soul is the witness to practice.

Sarvasākshih ātmā = The soul is the witness of all.

Nā syāt kutasākshi = One should not agree with evil as a witness.

Kutasākshino narake patanti = A false witness falls in hell.

Nakrashichan nāshayati samridharati wā = The witness does neither good nor bad.

Ātmanah pāpamātmaiva prakāshayati = A sinner unveils his own sins.

Prachchhanna pāpānām sākshino mahābhutāni = There are five witnesses to sins committed secretly. They are the five elements — the earth, water, fire, air and sky.

Vyawahāre antargatam ākārah suchayati = The face is the index of mind.

Ākārasanvaranam devānām shakyam = It is difficult even for gods to hide what the face is expressing.

Chorarājapurushebhya vittam rakshet = A king should protect the wealth from thief government officials (thieves and government officials).

Durdarshanā hi rājānah prajā nāshayati = A king who rarely appears before the public is finished.

Sudarshanā hi rājānah prajā = The people are pleased with the king who usually appears before them.

Nyāyayuktam rājānam mātaram manyte prajāh = A judicious king is treated as mother by the people.

Tādrishah sa rājā eha sukham tatah swargam āpnoti = A king loved by his people gets both the wordly and heavenly pleasures.

Chorānscha kantakāshcha satatam bināshayet = It is the duty of a king to keep on wiping out the thieves, the wicked and those who are obstacles.

Ahimsā lakshano dharmah = Non-violence is the characteristic of religion.

Nā samsārbhayam gyāwatām = A wise man has no fear.

Tapasā swargam āpnoti = One reaches the heaven with penance (austerity and good deeds).

SECTION – IV

Artha Shastra

Artha Shastra

Artha Shastra of Chanakya broadly deals with the following fourteen topics and areas related to kingdom, kingship, economy, politics, foreign policy and general mass:

1. King, his character and training, his duties and appointments of ministers
2. The duties of different officers of the state and its various activities
3. Law and the administration of justice
4. Suppression of crime and maintenance of law and order
5. Salaries and other related activities
6. Foreign policy and the constituent elements of a state
7. The way these six can be implemented
8. Natural calamities and the duties of the state
9. Details of preparations for war
10. Battle, battlefield and types of battle arrays

11. The works of a conqueror, his dealings with the king and chiefs
12. The ways and means of a weak king against a stronger one
13. The conquest of the enemy's fort by fighting
14. Occult practices

Chanakya has discussed six ways of dealing with neighbouring and distant kingdoms:

(i) ***Sandhi:*** making peace by treaty,

(ii) ***Vigrah:*** remaining hostile and busy in conventional war, secret war or proxy war, or an undeclared war and by keeping that kingdom busy in different problems,

(iii) ***Ãsana:*** to be watchful and silent and to do nothing,

(iv) ***Yana:*** preparing for war,

(v) ***Samāshraya:*** to seek protection from a stronger king, and

(vi) ***Dvaidhibhāva:*** making peace with a king to pursue the policy of hostility towards another

Chanakya was a different kind of thinker and has given some unusual and esoteric suggestions and many practicable solutions as well. He saw 'progress' and 'decline' in a different light. He said that the harm that one country brings to his enemy country is also progress, for that much less power and expense will be spent to defeat that country. It is just changing negative aspects into a positive gain. On the other hand, he said that the king should develop his state and direct the resources and power to embark on a conquest. It is true in the context of the modern open wars, cold wars and chemical wars. The countries show their power by WMDs (weapons for mass destruction) and nuclear weapons. The exhibition is different in the modern era and the secret weakening of the enemy and sometimes even of friends is always in progress.

Chanakya argued that those who help at the right moment are friends and those who do not are enemies, and the enemies must be eliminated. The enemy should not be allowed to progress and accumulate wealth or power. Chanakya wrote, "An enemy must be destroyed even at the cost of great loss of men, material, time and wealth." In addition to it, he also cautioned the kings that one should not submit or surrender to the enemy spinelessly, nor one should foolishly sacrifice oneself and one's soldiers and people for no solid gain. One must avoid both the extremes. One should follow such a balanced policy so as to survive the day to regain strength during the night full of darkness to return again to the battlefield in the brightness of another morning to fight again for a comprehensive win. One must adopt a prudent course and a calculated strategy to weave a tightening web around the enemy for sure success. After regaining the breath and strength, the king should set out a campaign against the enemy and wisely choose the time of attack when all the forces of the enemy are not mobilised.

Chanakya showed eight different factors which have great bearing on the success or failure of a campaign. One should consider well regarding all of them before thinking to attack. An indepth and balanced analysis helps a king take correct decision. But Chanakya laid stress that once the decision is taken and the campaign is on, then it must be followed to its logical end steadfastly and it should in no case be stopped in the middle. The eight factors are the following:

Power of one's own and the enemy must be assessed before planning a campaign or even before thinking to attack. It is simply suicidal to attack a strong opponent without knowing his power. Here, power to him is not only the military power but also the moral and intellectual power of the other king.

Place of the campaign also has its significance and a battle can be won or lost only by the suitable or non-suitable battlefield or the terrain.

Time is another major factor which decides the fate of a campaign. If the time suits then it is alright but if it is otherwise then the result is declared before the actual battle.

The type of troops should be decided according to the strength, troops and season.

Internal revolt finishes and completely erases one, whether a weak or a strong king or an ordinary person.

Expectations must be assessed at the time of planning. If there is no chance or no hope for a greater gain then the campaign should be nipped in the bud.

Extent of losses should also be calculated to come to the right figure of net gain or loss.

A king must guard himself against the **possibility of treachery**, which ruins not only the campaign but the king and his subjects too.

In the same breath, Chanakya gave the advice that the king must behave in the similar fashion, whether he wins or loses. He should neither make a show of the win nor weep at the loss.

Naturally, peace and truce or treaty with an enemy cannot be permanent. It must be made purely on a temporary basis to regain the lost breath and fallen sword. The moment the breath returns and the sword comes in grip, one should endeavour hard to eliminate the enemy for ever. Enemies are synonyms of sleepless nights, pain, suffering, destruction and miserable life.

Regarding treaties between the states, Chanakya wrote that non-intervention, negotiating a peace-treaty and making peace by giving a hostage were the same thing. They had similar aims to create confidence between two warring kings. He did not support hostages. On the other hand he stressed on the words, oaths and promises of the kings. Such things were more stable. He had another reason for it. He thought that the hostages could liberate themselves by their own efforts or with the help of other clandestine agents adopting various disguises, using entertainers, or attendants which might create different serious problems, for the hostages would bent upon taking revenge.

Regarding the choice of allies, he expressed his views that one should select an ally who is unable to control. The allies must be temporary and one should be kept as an ally till one helps. The day he fails to help, he should be omitted from the list of allies. Between the kings, the real test of friendship is help. He made distinction between constant ally and temporary ally. A constant ally was he who regularly rendered small help. He should be preferred over temporary ally who gave substantial help. The latter might be afraid of giving such helps in future also or he might expect adequate return in lieu thereof. So he can prove to be dangerous.

In his opinion that ally was better who rendered help in the form of money and kind than the one who offered troops. The troops could be used once in a while and would incur expenses while help in cash and kind could be utilised in many ways for different ends. Money gave flexibility and kept the options open.

The welfare of a state depended heavily on strong and active foreign policy. It also depended on the honest endeavour of the state to promote welfare of the people because the strength of a state came from its people. They were the real strength, while the wealth and power of the king was limited. The people ceaselessly supplied him men, material and other backups.

SECTION – V

Conclusion

The Incomparable Chanakya

Chanakya was a reputed thinker and a man of fast and lasting action, a strict teacher and a fair administrator, an immaculate strategist and a manipulator, a dexterous planner and an extraordinary executive, a destructive force and a creative energy, rational and highly emotional, an annihilator of a kingdom and a creator of a dynasty, he was always superb and performed his works with perfection. He did everything with his mental power. He was an *acharya* just out of the university after teaching for a few years, when he took the most feared vow to demolish the Nand Dynasty. He had left the profession of teaching to share his wisdom for the good of the society. The Nand Dynasty was either sucking the people dry or throwing them into luxury and unscrupulous works. It was ruinous for the society and the country. He demolished it with character and grace. He had no money, no power, no post and no army, yet with his mental ability and determined effort, he created an emperor out of a village child, raised a big, capable and well-furnished army and accomplished an impossible task. He was the man to best realise the power of wisdom and an exemplary writer to declare, 'only he is powerful who has wisdom — *buddhiryasya balam tasya nirbuddhestu kuto balam*'.

That single and simple event changed the history of India, that single Brahmin changed the life and attitude of the millions of men in every century down the ages. With his own effort, he has now become as high as a mountain which cannot be scaled, a deep sea which cannot be fathomed, a blowing wind which cannot be checked and the purest human being who cannot be won. Chanakya is bigger than a *shal* tree, fertile as a basin, secure as a cave and illuminating as sunrays. He is worshipped and feared at the same time. It is the living force of the man who worked and activated countless volcanic transformers some two thousand five hundred years ago.

Chanakya was not a person who could please others, or give pleasure to anyone. He was a very tough person. He always commented that life was not easy and one should never wish or try to lead an easy life. Life was the greatest boon. Every moment of it should be utilised for betterment, growth, perfection and salvation. Such purification of human nature and selfless deeds were essential. Naturally, he was all out for wisdom, purification, action, dutifulness and righteousness.

Where on the one hand, Chanakya generated fear; on the other hand, he also created awe. He hurled a teacher's long thin stick which striked hard and the ensuing pain lasted. In the present scenario, when the corrupt are becoming more powerful, and there is virtually no punishment for crimes, and in numerous cases, the criminals and degenerated people are honoured and venerated, a Chanakya is needed to overhaul the system, to deal sternly with the people and problems, to give severe punishment to bring changes for a better society and kingdom to live in. In one *sutra*, he mentioned that one should not live in a kingdom where there is terror, '*anupadrawam deshamāwaset*'. Today, the whole world is in the grip of terror. There is no place worth living. There is not a single country which has peace and there is no single profession which is not corrupt. All are selfish and ready to commit any type of crime for personal gain. There is no check on immoral act and degeneration of the once sublime human life. Thus, a Chanakya is badly required to amend the existing system.

Apart from the fear that he generated, Chanakya also taught fearlessness. Whenever a door opens, a criminal imagines the arrival of police. He gets no peace. In such a condition, all the means of pleasure and luxury become meaningless. It is the real meaning of life. He advocated a fearless life which comes the hard way. The worst are not afraid of the insults, the conscious are not afraid of unemployment, the wise are not afraid of falls, and those who have been honest and dutiful are not afraid of death.

Nāstya mānabhayam anāryasya
Nā chetanwattām britibhayam
Nā jeetendriyānām vishayabhayam
Nā kritārthānām maranbhayam

That fearless individual is the man who steadily grows and ascends up on the ladder of wisdom, action, fame and respect, and never steps back.

Dharma was the most important thing for Chanakya. *Dharma* signifies 'righteousness and one's duty towards self, family, society, the earth and the universal order'. *Artha* follows *Dharma*. *Artha* which literally means wealth has a much wider significance in Indian context. It is not only the maintenance of law and order and administrative machinery that is important, in fact the maintenance of the self, the body, its machinery and family and social order are equally important. Chanakya saw and felt all and tried his best to make others see and feel it. Here lies his unparalleled success and greatness. He did nothing for the selfish self; he did everything for the society and the kingdom. He ensured the protection of the king, security to the kingdom and safety and prosperity to the people. He had great inclination for democratic values.

There are various facets and phases in the life of Chanakya in which 'known wisdom and imperceptible execution' are at the top, though he faced many reversals and upheavals. It is difficult for anyone to match even a single facet of his life. In fact, many combined together cannot match Chanakya. Thus, it is obvious that Chanakya is incomparable.

But Chanakya is quite comprehensible. He is among the easiest to understand and among very difficult to follow. If '*sandhi*' (which can be called 'synapse' if a term from medical science is applied to grammar) is separated and the words are written separately then he would prove to be the simplest writer on the most general and intricate subjects and problems.

He is taken as 'angry, prejudiced and stubborn'. He had a solid and profitable reason behind his plans and implemented them in such a way, at such moments and for such causes that he gained a lot from out of his anger, prejudice and stubbornness. It is also rare among the rarest in human history. Anyone with these traits is surely to get ruined, but Chanakya thrived with them. He was a practical man of the soil and with unheard of successes, he became an idea, a precept and a philosophy; he did not remain a man.

Chanakya must be intently and thoroughly read and his teachings must be followed rigorously, boldly, painfully and sincerely for better vision, sure success and greater gain.